Spinoza and Moral Freedom

SUNY Series in Philosophy
Robert C. Neville, Editor

SPINOZA AND MORAL FREEDOM

S. Paul Kashap

State University of New York Press

Published by
State University of New York Press, Albany

Printed in the United States of America

For information, address State University of New York Press, State University Plaza, Albany, N.Y., 12246

Library of Congress Cataloging in Publication Data

Kashap, S. Paul.
Spinoza and moral freedom.

(SUNY series in philosophy)
"References to Spinoza's works": p.
Includes index.
1. Spinoza, Benedictus de, 1632-1677. 2. Free will and determinism—History—17th century. 3. Ethics, Modern—17th century. I. Title. II. Series.
B3999.F8K37 1987 170 86-30210
ISBN 0-88706-529-5
ISBN 0-88706-530-9 (pbk.)

10 9 8 7 6 5 4 3 2 1

To Nancy

Contents

Preface

While most writers on Spinoza seem to take it for granted that Spinoza's metaphysics does not allow for moral freedom, no one has adequately examined what his stand on this important issue is. In this book I examine the topic in detail through analysis, interpretation, and reconstruction of Spinoza's concepts of 'substance' (God), 'ideas,' 'action,' 'cause,' and 'freedom.,'

The rationale for the structure and content of the book is as follows: Any serious student of Spinoza comes to recognize that an adequate account of Spinoza's views on ethics and his philosophy of freedom demands a clear and plausible account of his concept of substance (or God) and his concept of true ideas, knowledge, or understanding. Spinoza's concept of action is logically related to true ideas; and freedom consists of the performance of actions as they relate to ideas that are true. Yet, for Spinoza, there is a sense in which a human being's existence depends upon factors over which he or she has no control. This makes it incumbent upon a commentator to show (1) what kind of relation Spinoza envisages between these ultimate factors and a person's existence, and (2) what kind of factors allow the possibility of applying the notion of freedom to man (that is, 'freedom' in the sense that we ordinarily understand it in speaking of moral freedom, and 'freedom' in the sense that Spinoza considers the most significant sense of human freedom). It is therefore important to articulate and clarify Spinoza's notions of God, ideas, action, and cause, in an effort to understand his views on freedom.

This explication of a portion of Spinoza's metaphysics is presented such that every subsequent chapter assumes the knowledge of the contents of the preceding ones. The first chapter is concerned with clarifying Spinoza's concept of substance and the sense of 'existence' applicable to God; it describes the relation between God, attributes, and modes; and it ends with an explanation of the sense of freedom as it applies to God, and the suggestion that this sense of freedom is not to be confused with freedom of the will.

The second chapter examines and analyzes Spinoza's use of the term 'idea' in order to clarify his sense of rational knowledge, understanding, or true ideas, as they relate to the human mind.

The third chapter is an analysis of Spinoza's notion of action and its relation to (a) the truth and adequacy of ideas, (b) his concept of desire (*cupiditas*), (c) the interconnection between mind and body, and (d) the distinction between reasons and causes.

The fourth chapter analyzes the sense in which Spinoza holds God to be the ultimate causal factor in the existence of things in the common order of nature, and it also analyzes the notions of contingency and possibility as Spinoza understood them, and their implications for the thesis of determinism.

The last chapter examines what precisely Spinoza was deny ing when he is understood to have denied freedom of the will, what he meant by freedom as it applies to man, and whether this idea of freedom is compatible with the acceptance of moral distinctions that we normally make in speaking of the freedom to choose.

I could have expanded the scope of this book by comparing and contrasting Spinoza's views with those of Descartes and Leibniz, as has been done in several other books (e.g., those by Errol Harris, Henry Allison, or Stuart Hampshire), but this was not my intent here.

This book is different from most others in that, while it does deal with certain salient features of Spinoza's metaphysics and theory of knowledge, I examine these concepts only insofar as I consider them relevant to reconstructing his stand on the issue of moral freedom.

The hero of my account is Spinoza, and no one else. I have him speak for himself. My aim is to make Spinoza intelligible in the way he would have wished to be understood, that is, not through reference to anyone else. This is not a book on the history of Spinoza's philosophy but on the philosophy of Spinoza. If I could do away with the few references to Descartes and Leibniz, I would be pleased to do so. Incidental references to them, however, are consistent with the aim of this book. I wish to show that Spinoza can be understood on his own, and that, indeed, he must be understood independently of anyone else's thought if he is not to be misunderstood.

This leads to another point: My concern is with the issue of moral freedom in Spinoza and not socio-political freedom. The latter deserves separate study. It cannot be mentioned or dealt with in a couple of paragraphs, a couple of pages, or even a whole chapter; it requires a whole manuscript to itself, and is not my concern in this book.

I have carefully selected only those passages and statements from Spinoza's earlier works and correspondence which are relevant to clarifying and understanding the statements and views expressed in his most mature and finished work, the *Ethics*. The *Ethics* is a very compressed work. Whenever, therefore, I have found a discursive passage elsewhere in his writings which uses more, and at times different words to say what is expressed more tersely in the *Ethics,* I use it to perform an explanatory function. In that sense all his works are, so to say, "spread out on the table," but they are referred to with circumspection and discrimination, so that they may serve to reconstruct his thought.

I am indebted to Professors Roderick Chisholm, David Savan, Maurice Natanson, and Arne Naess for reading earlier drafts and for their encouragement, and to Albert Hofstadter for offering helpful comments on the contents of a chapter. I am grateful to Wallace Matson for extremely valuable comments on the whole of an earlier draft; to my colleague, W. Emmanuel Abraham, for his help with the final copy; and to the anonymous readers of the State University of New York Press for their comments.

I must also acknowledge my debt to Sir Stuart Hampshire with whom I began my study of Spinoza at Oxford more than a quarter of a century ago; and to Professor H. Paul Grice. Both of them through their writings have, in diverse ways, influenced my own thinking about Spinoza.

I am grateful to Shelley Starr who typed an earlier draft from a handwritten manuscript, to Chris LeBoeuf for being good tempered while making innumerable changes in a series of drafts, and to Peg McCray, Valerie Wells, and Cheryl Van De Veer, of the University of California Word Processing Center, for producing the final computer copy.

Thanks to Janet Burton and Evelyn Kane for editing, and

special thanks to Philip Kashap whose editorial assistance has made the book more readable, and to Dr. Bruce Kermott for devoting time in preparing the index.

My greatest debts are to my wife, Nancy Kashap, whose unfailing help at every step of the way made this work possible.

Parts of Chapter Two were published in *Spinoza: New Perspectives*, edited by Robert W. Shahan and J. I. Biro (University of Oklahoma Press 1978), and are reproduced here with permission of the Director.

Parts of Chapter Three were originally published in *Studies in Spinoza*, edited by S. Paul Kashap (the Regents of the University of California, 1972), and are reproduced here with permission of the University of California Press.

References to Spinoza's Works

E — *Ethics.* References to Ethics follow the numbers of Parts, Propositions, Definitions, Corollaries, Scholia, and Demonstrations as they occur in Volume I of the Van Vloten and Land edition of Spinoza's works in four volumes. (*E* I, A4 = part I, axiom 4, *E* II, 13 C = part II, proposition 13, corollary; *E* III, 28 S = part III, proposition 28, scholium; *E* IV, D3 = part IV, definition 3; *E* V, 35 D = part V, proposition 35, demonstration).

DIE — *Tractatus de Intellectus Emendatione* (Treatise on the Improvement of the Understanding). Section and passage numbers refer to the convenient and clear arrangement in A. Boyle's translation.

ST — *Short Treatise on God, Man and His Well-Being,* translated by A. Wolf.

Ep — *Epistolae.* In *Correspondence of Spinoza;* numeration follows A. Wolf's translation.

TPT

Tractatus Theologico-Politicus (Theological-Political Treatise).

TP

Tractatus Politicus (Political Treatise).

Several English translations of Spinoza's works were consulted along with the Van Vloten edition. Almost all available translations were found disappointingly inadequate. The only exceptions were A.G. Wernham's *The Political Works of Spinoza* and White and Sterling's translation of the *Ethics*. Even the latter was inadequate in many places, and, on the occasions when translations were found philosophically misleading, I provided my own version.

Translations of Descartes's works are taken almost verbatim from E. S. Haldane and G. R. T. Ross, *The Philosophical Works of Descartes*

Chapter One

Substance

1.1

One of the most fundamental notions in Spinoza's thought is that there is an inherent distinction between things that are dependent and things that are independent. The term 'things' is to be taken in a neutral sense to signify not merely physical objects but also thoughts or ideas and anything else that may be said to exist. The notions of 'dependence' and 'independence' themselves, when carefully considered, reveal an interesting complexity. What is meant by them at this stage is that for a thing to be dependent is for it to be dependent on something other than itself for its existence, reality or being. So that it is in principle impossible for a thing to belong to the class of dependent things without implying, in the strictest sense, that in the explanation of its existence, reference to things other than itself must be involved and required. In contrast with this, for a thing to be independent is for it not to depend for its existence, its reality, or its being on anything other than (or external to) itself.

These two classes or categories of things are mutually exclusive, in the sense that no thing that belongs to one category can (logically) belong to the other without forfeiting the applicability of the term 'dependent' or 'independent' with respect to it. This distinction is at once logical or conceptual, as well as ontological. That is to say, whatever may exist can be thought of as belonging only to one or the other of these two classes. That which belongs to neither one nor the other can neither be thought or nor can it exist in any intelligible sense of 'exist'.

It is this distinction between dependent and independent things which is related to the idea expressed by Spinoza in the statements, "Everything which is, is either in itself or in another"(*E* I, A1); and, "That which cannot be conceived through another must be conceived through itself" (*E* I, A2). It is this same distinction that is expressed when he says, "Of each existing thing there must necessarily be a positive cause through which it exists" (*Ep* 34). That is to say, either a thing depends for its existence on a cause that is within itself, or it depends for its existence on a cause outside itself. As Spinoza puts it in the same letter, "This cause must be placed either in the nature and the definition of the thing itself . . . or outside the thing." He restates this point by saying that "Of every existing thing there is some certain cause by reason of which it exists" (i.e., which explains why it exists); and, "This cause by reason of which a thing exists, must either be contained in the nature itself and definition of the existing thing (simply because it pertains to the nature of the thing to exist), or it must exist outside the thing" (*E* I, 8S2).

1.2

The introduction of the term 'definition' here is significant. For Spinoza there seems to be only one sense in which a definition of anything can be 'proper' or 'true' definition. The true definition of a thing is a statement such that it "includes nothing but the simple nature of the thing defined" (*Ep* 34). In the *Ethics* (I, P8S2) he puts the same idea more clearly. There he states, "[T]he true definition of anything neither involves nor expresses anything except the nature of the thing defined." It is because the definition of a thing gives expression to the inmost essence or nature of the thing in question that the statement about the properties of that thing, insofar as these properties must follow from its essential nature, can be said to follow from the thing's definition. The properties of a thing, being necessarily related to the nature of a thing, can be said to be deducible from the statement of the nature or essence of the thing. For this reason it makes sense for Spinoza to say that an idea or conception that is expressed in the definition of a thing "should be such that all the properties [i.e., the statement of the properties], of that thing can be deduced [i.e., inferred] from it" (*DIE* 96). So a definition for Spinoza is clearly an expression in language of what he calls elsewhere "the inmost essence of a thing" (*DIE* 95).

The type of definition Spinoza recognizes as a 'true' definition is known as a 'real' definition, distinct from any other kind, such as stipulative, lexicographical, technical, and so on. Spinoza seems to have reasons for selecting this kind of definition as the 'true' definition. He points out in his *Treatise on the Improvement of the Understanding* that to understand anything is to "apprehend things without error" (*DIE* 16); to think clearly, to distinguish between different kinds of things and to grasp their essential nature and character. The highest achievement or the 'chief good' for a human being would be for him or her to entertain only those thoughts or ideas that reflect the nature of the world as it is. If every idea in one's mind were correlated to the nature of reality as it truly is, then the whole system of thoughts or ideas thus formed would constitute a kind of unity between the mind and whatever is the case in the universe. Consequently, the highest human achievement would consist, as he puts it, "in attaining or arriving at this union between the mind and the whole of nature" (*DIE* 13).

1.3

There are various synonyms for the terms 'dependent' and 'independent' in Spinoza's thought. A dependent thing is one that is 'finite', whose existence is limited, caused or created by something other than itself. It is therefore called 'in another' and 'conceived though another' thing. On the other hand, an independent thing is one that is 'infinite', not caused by another outside itself. It is self-existent, *causa sui*, uncreated. It is therefore called 'in itself' and 'conceived though itself'.

These two classes or categories of things, as noted earlier, are mutually exclusive, in that anything that belongs to one category cannot belong to the other. Hence the rules that must be observed in giving expression to the nature of a dependent thing, in the statement of its definition, will have to differ from those that are to be observed in giving expression to the nature of a thing that is independent. Failure to observe these rules will inevitably lead to mistaking a thing belonging to one category for a thing belonging to another, and consequently to a general confusion in understanding the true nature of things as they essentially are.

Accordingly, Spinoza suggests (*DIE* 96) that if the thing to be defined is a dependent or a created thing then its definition must specify the conditions or factors which explain how it came to be. (i.e., its immediate or proximate cause). The inmost essence of a thing that depends for its existence on conditions external to itself consists precisely in those conditions without which it could not be produced, or come to be what it is. Furthermore, once the essential conditions for its production have been specified then it should be possible to infer all the characteristics or properties of a thing from such a definition. This second suggestion, it should be noted, clearly involves an unfolding of the very nature of the thing that is being defined. It would be, in principle, impossible for the thing defined, once produced, to fail to exhibit the properties or characteristics typical of it. In order to make sure that the definition is precisely that of the specific thing concerned, the properties or characteristics of the thing must be distinguished from the causal conditions that bring the thing about. The properties of a thing must, of course, follow from its nature and hence must be inferred from the statement of the definition. This does not mean that the properties which follow from the nature of the thing, and hence which must also be deducible from the definitions, are identical with the casual conditions of its existence. The conditions of a thing's existence are, indeed, inseparable from the properties that belong to it, yet the two are logically distinct. The causal conditions, in other words, without which a thing could not exist, are not the same as the characteristics it must have once it is brought into existence.

Spinoza appears to clarify this point by means of an illustration (*DIE* 95). Suppose that a circle is defined as a figure, such that all straight lines drawn from the center to the circumference are equal. Now this definition clearly does not explain how a figure of a circle is made or produced; it does not explain the inmost essence of a circle as a dependent thing by mentioning the immediate condition or proximate cause of its being a circle rather than any other figure. It already assumes the reality or existence of a circle and expresses one of its properties. So according to Spinoza's suggestion (*DIE* 96), the proper and true definition of a circle would be that it is a figure described by a straight line whereof one end is fixed and the other is free. This clearly comprehends the proximate cause and states how the figure is brought about, and hence constitutes a proper definition. What is defined in this example is an abstract thing, which may not be, Spinoza observes, of much importance. The rule that is followed here is of much greater importance "in the case of physical beings and realities"; for, as Spinoza tells us, "the properties of things are not understood so long as their essences are unknown" (*DIE* 95). Evidently by the 'essence' of a created or a dependent thing Spinoza here means the immediate causal conditions which bring the thing about, or which make it exist. Once a thing comes into existence, however, then its 'essence' or 'nature' consists in those properties which necessarily follow from its existence as distinct from those which are merely accidental. This second sense of 'essence', which refers to a thing's nature after it has come into existence, is not, according to Spinoza, what belongs in the statement of a proper or true definition of a created thing. These two senses of the term 'essence' are to be kept distinct. The essential properties that follow once the thing exists are not to be confused with the causal conditions that bring a thing into existence.

A thing that is dependent for its existence on external causal conditions is necessarily an effect of those conditions. To understand anything which is an effect would require understanding or knowing the causes that bring it about; hence Spinoza's observation that "the knowledge of an effect depends upon and involves the knowledge of its cause" (*E* I, A4). Our understanding of the nature of a dependent thing increases, in fact, with an increase in our comprehension of the conditions and factors that bring it about (*DIE* 92). If one follows this train of thinking with respect to the definition of a dependent thing, then one might say that since each dependent thing depends for its existence on other conditions and factors—which themselves would depend for their existence on still other conditions and factors—we shall be led to an infinite regress of causal conditions, each depending for its existence on some others of the same category. Thus everything that exists would belong to one single category, namely, the category of dependent things. The question then arises as to how the chain began. Assuming there is a first cause, what kinds of conditions and factors explain the existence of the first link in the chain of dependent causal conditions? Spinoza's division of everything that exists into the categories of 'dependent thing' or 'independent thing' is meant to provide an answer to this perplexing and difficult question.

The problem, as Spinoza sees it, is that by merely tracing each effect to its cause and that cause to another cause indefinitely, we cannot provide a satisfactory answer to the question of the character or nature of the first cause so long as the first cause is conceived as a member within the series of causes and effects. The same question that we ask about any member of the cause-effect series can be asked about the first member in that series, in the fashion in which children sometimes tend to ask "Who made God?" The recourse to the notion of the first cause as God is taken precisely to put a stop to the infinite regression of dependent causal series by claiming that the infinite regression is impossible.

1.4

Spinoza's own solution to the problem concerning the impossibility of infinite regression is expressed with some clarity towards the end of an important letter he wrote to Meyer (*Ep* 12). There he restates the well-known argument of infinite regression as follows: "If there is an infinite regression of causes, then all things which exist will be things that have been caused. But it cannot pertain to anything that has been caused that it should necessarily exist in virtue of its own nature. Therefore there is in Nature nothing to whose essence it pertains that it should exist necessarily. But this is absurd." Spinoza's response is significant and important. He observes that "the force of the argument lies not in the idea that . . . a regression of causes to infinity is impossible, but only in the impossibility of supposing that things which do not exist necessarily in virtue of their own nature, are not determine to existence by something which does exist necessarily in virtue of its own nature, and which is a cause, not an effect (*Ep* 12).

Here Spinoza has drawn our attention to the true nature of the 'first cause' by making a distinction between the notions of 'dependent thing' and 'independent thing', and by showing that it is impossible to conceive of the nature of the first cause as an independent reality if it is conceived as a member, and transient cause, of an infinite chain of causes and effects. If the first cause is thought of as the first link in the endless duration of causal processes, then it is not only impossible to avoid the question as to what caused the first cause, but it also involves misapprehending the character of a thing that is independent of, and unconditioned by, any causes outside itself. In other words, a thing that is independent is not the kind of thing whose existence could be, or be required to be, explained by reference to causes outside itself. It is *causa sui* (*E*I, D1), not in the sense that it brought itself about—as though something which did not exist could yet operate in such a way as to bring itself into existence—but that it is that which has no cause at all,[1] precisely because it is not a dependent thing but a thing that is independent, unconditioned, infinite.

Perhaps, now it is possible to see why Spinoza should state that an independent thing is not only *causa sui* (*E*I, D1) but, being such, it must be in itself and hence conceived through itself. Since its very nature is such that it is "in itself," its conception or definition "does not need the conception of another thing from which it must be formed." This is the kind of reality for which Spinoza uses the term 'substance' in the *Ethics* (I D3) where he says that 'substance' is "that which is in itself and is conceived though itself; in other words, that the conception of which does not need the conception of another thing from which it must be formed."

1.5

A word of caution is in place here. Although Spinoza's definitions were 'real' definitions, there is yet a considerable amount of ambiguity involved in the character of a real definition.[2] The point about a real definition is that it purports to express or define the nature of the thing that a word stands for, rather than the word itself. Nevertheless, even a real definition is inevitably expressed

[1]Cf. A. Wolf, *ST,* p. 172.

[2]See my review of E.E. Harris's *Salvation From Despair: A Reappraisal of Spinoza's Philosophy,* in *Man and World,* Vol. 9, No. 4, pp. 435–451.

in words. The danger is in believing that once we understand the meaning of the words, and the sentences in which a real definition is expressed, we shall have understood the nature of the thing involved in a real definition. The matter is not that simple. No matter how accurately one may comprehend the meanings of words, the grammatical and syntactical rules of the language of which they form a part, and the context of their use, one may yet fail to understand the nature of the thing that is the subject of a real definition.

Ultimately, even after a real definition is provided, and the meaning of the sentence through which it is expressed is understood, what is required is a further insight—to see, in a curious, but significant sense, that it does have an application. A real definition functions, at best, only as a pointer which draws one's attention to, or hints at the reality of the thing in question. There is no guarantee that whoever understands the meaning of a statement of definition in a given language will also have understood the nature of the thing that was being thus defined.

Consider Spinoza's statement "God is eternal, or all His attributes are eternal" (*E* I, 19). In the demonstration of this proposition he says, "For God is substance, which necessarily exists, that is to say, to whose nature it pertains to exist, or (which is the same thing) from the definition of which it follows that it exists, and therefore is eternal." From what has been said about the nature of things that are independent, it is fairly clear that 'substance' is regarded by Spinoza as such a thing; and God is claimed to be identical with substance as well as with all the attributes that characterize its reality or being. Since a thing that is independent does not need causes outside itself in order to ex plain its being, its existence or being follows from its own nature. It exists not because there is something else that brings it about, but solely by virtue of its own essence. Its essence, in fact, is identical with its existence or reality. This is to say that "its essence necessarily involves existence" (*E* I, 7D). Only a reality "without beginning or end" and whose existence cannot be explained by reference to anything that belongs to the category of dependent things, is to be thought of properly as eternal.

1.6

Now if the notion of 'definition' were to be conceived in such a way that words alone were capable of being defined, then nothing would appear to follow from Spinoza's 'definition' of 'substance', except that he has decided, or stipulated, or is instituting a convention, to use the word in such a way that its equivalent(s) can also be used. It is quite obvious that the referent of a word or an expression cannot be brought into existence by virtue of a mere act of referring or by a decision to use a word as a sutstantive term.

Moreover, it would be highly misleading to take Spinoza as merely saying "By the word 'God' I mean what I mean by the words 'substance' or 'infinite attributes'." Spinoza's definitions characteristically begin with "By . . . I understand . . . " (*Per intelligo id).* The Latin term *intelligo* has among its meanings the sense of 'to take or suppose to mean' as has the English term 'to understand'. This sense is reinforced by the use of the personal pronoun 'I' (i.e., "I take this word to mean such and such"). There is little doubt that Spinoza is doing this; but this is not all that he is doing. He is also using words and sentences that have meaning to *point to the nature* of a thing or reality, and not merely setting up or legislating arbitrary conventions for the use of these words. It may be that our tendency to take him to be doing the latter, entailed by the acceptance of the notion of definition as confined to words, leads to the idea that surely if Spinoza could form his own linguistic conventions, so could anyone else. Others may mean and have meant by 'substance' something quite different from what he means by it. No philosopher can have an exclusive right to lay down the rule that the words 'substance', or 'attribute', or 'mode' must mean what he stipulates them to mean. To approach Spinoza with this sort of argument, however, is to fail to understand him from the very start. It is the result of the ambiguity that is involved in the nature of a real definition in which words and sentences are used to talk about things that are not themselves linguistic but extra-linguistic.

1.7

Another point with regard to Spinoza's use of 'substance' or 'God' is that there is hardly any way to justify the belief that he is using these terms as proper names,[3] in either their primary or descriptive function. The primary function of a proper name is to refer to an individual thing or a person so that the thing named or described can be picked out and identified as the one to which the name or the description applies. Substance or God, as Spinoza points out in so many ways,[4] cannot be a finite individual like man, nor can human attributes have any place in God. In fact Spinoza does not even think it appropriate to say that God is one or single (*Ep* 50).

Spinoza's reason for this are that we think of things as one or more, in terms of numbers, only after they have been subsumed under a common class. For example, a person holding a

---

[3]Cf. H.F Hallet's review of R.L. Saw's *The Vindication of Metaphysics* in *Philosophy* 1952, p. 175. Hallet rightly observes that in Spinoza "'God' is not a proper name."

[4]Cf. *E* I, S2; *Ep* 21,23,54,56.

penny and a dollar will not think of calling them two unless he can call both of them by the same name, such as pieces of money, or coins or physical objects. Nothing can be called one or single (as if to answer the question how many?) unless some other thing has been conceived which shares something in common with it and in that respect belongs to the same category. God is unique in that it is *causa sui* and does not have or does not need a cause outside itself to explain its existence; or, which is the same thing, it is in God's nature to be or to exist, there being nothing which falls in the same class: "He who calls God one or single has no true idea of God, or is speaking of Him inappropriately" (*E*p 50).

Spinoza's reasons for saying that the notion of singularity or number cannot be applicable to God seem quite distinct from the point that Frege was trying to make in showing how Spinoza could have arrived at the concept of number without abstracting it from a number of objects.[5] To say that God is unique, or the only reality of its kind, is surely not to say how many Gods there are, but rather to direct attention to the fact that such a question is improper when asked with respect to 'substance' or God.[6]

---

[5]Cf. *Foundations of Arithmetic,* trans. by J.L. Austin (Oxford: Oxford University Press, 1950), p. 62.

[6]Parkinson's observation (see *Spinoza's Theory of Knowledge* (Oxford: 1954) p. 63) that Spinoza's demonstrations in the *Ethics* to show that God is single, and his claim that it is inappropriate to say God is one or single, seem to involve Spinoza in a contradiction, appears to me much too hasty a characterization of Spinoza's position. To understand him correctly is to see that his attempts to show that there can be only one substance or God is his way of drawing attention to the uniqueness of God or substance. God is unlike any other thing in that it is not and cannot be dependent upon anything other than its own nature or essence to be or to exist. This is not to say, however, how many Gods there are.

A similar point is made by P.T. Geach (see *Reason and Reality,* London: Macmillan, 1972, p. 21) when he points out that only that which can be identified, individuated and discriminated can be counted. The implication is that

Now if the notion of singularity or numerical individuality cannot appropriately be applied to God, then it is difficult to see how 'God' can be said to be a 'proper name', or the definition of God a 'description' of God, in the sense in which the 'proper name' in its primary or descriptive function makes it possible to identify and pick out or individuate the thing named from among the things presented to one's experience in the world.

Furthermore, Spinoza's 'substance' and 'God' do not have as their reference a historical, mythical or fictitious entity capable of being identified or described in the way one may identify or describe, for instance, the present Queen of England, Zeus, or Hamlet. Spinoza's statement "God or substance consisting of infinite attributes . . . necessarily exists" (*E* I, P11) cannot correctly be taken as a description of God or substance, but only as an expression which indicates the nature of the reality referred to by the use of the word 'God'. Properly speaking, God cannot be described, but can only be understood or conceived and in that sense known. This is what Spinoza seems to imply in his answer to Boxel when he writes, "To your question whether I have as clear an idea of God as I have of a triangle, I shall answer No. For we cannot imagine God, but we can, indeed, conceive Him" (*Ep* 56).

1.8

A point not often kept in mind, but which is extremely important, is that the meaning of the term 'exist' when Spinoza says 'God . . . exists' is entirely different from its meaning when existence is asserted of an individual or particular thing or object in history or fiction or in the common order of nature which Russell

since God is not the kind of reality that can be individuated, discriminated, identified or picked out, it is not something to which the notion of one or many can be applicable.

calls 'the real world'. The whole question of whether 'existence' is or is not a genuine predicate is beside the point here. What is significant to note is that for Spinoza the existence or actuality of things is to be conceived in two ways (*E* V, 29S). One of these ways corresponds to what we normally understand when we consider things existing as spatio-temporal objects in relation of a fixed time and place. The other sense involves conceiving existence, as he says, "under the form of eternity. . . ." This second sense is quite distinct from the first. It cannot be denied that the terms 'substance' and 'God' function as grammatical subjects in many of Spinoza's statements, including their definitions. They are also used as referring expressions. And it is also clear that their purported reference is not an individual person or a thing in the spatio-temporal order, nor is it a name of an object in the so-called phenomenal world of sense experience or in the physical world governed by natural laws. One may be inclined to accept the view that referring expressions can be used to refer to anything of any category or type whether existing or nonexisting. To know what one is referring to or speaking about is not the same as to know that there exists some thing to which one is referring. One may want or intend to refer to something which does not actually exist but is an imaginary or fictitious or logically impossible object. The linguistic act of referring is the same in each case and to that extent noncommittal in respect of existence.[7]

The question arises whether there is any criterion to determine whether a referring expression does have an actually existing thing as its object or reference as distinct from a nonexisting thing. A short answer given to this could be that any expression

---

[7]Cf. S. Hampshire, "Identification and Existence," *Contemporary British Philosophy,* Third Series, Ed. H.D. Lewis. London, Allen & Unwin, 1956, pp. 202–204.

or phrase when used referentially to stand for something that actually exists, must be such that it is used to make an identification. What is meant by this is that the explication of the reference or the answer the speaker would give to the question "What are you referring to?" is "that thing which looks like such and such", said in the presence of the object, where the reference of 'this' or 'that' is in this way an extra-linguistic reference. It is only when the referring expression can be said to stand for something directly identifiable in this way that it can be said to stand for something which actually exists.[8]

I am not suggesting that there is anything wrong with this criterion, but it does have limitations. It assumes that anything that can be said to exist actually can exist only as belonging to the world of spatio-temporal order given to sense experience. This is precisely the contention that Spinoza appears to be rejecting in making a distinction between two ways in which things can be actual or exist. The criterion of identification that is applied in determining the actual existence of the object of a referring expression in the common order of nature could not be applied to determine the actuality of the objects of referring expressions such as 'substance' and 'God' which belong to an altogether different logical type. This distinction is intimately connected with the fundamental distinction that Spinoza makes between independent things and dependent things.

It is of crucial importance, therefore, to understand that the existence of things in the common order of nature and the existence of substance or God are distinct in kind. Spinoza constantly reminds us of this distinction in many different ways.

Consider his statements, "The existence of God and His es-

---

[8]Ibid.

sence are one and the same thing" (*E* I, 20), and, "The essence of things produced by God does not involve existence" (*E* I, 24). These two propositions, taken together with Spinoza's statement to the effect that an individual thing or a thing which is finite or dependent must have other finite or dependent things as their causal conditions of existence (*E* I, 28; *E* II, 9D; *E* II, 30D and *E* II, 31D), would indicate that what he calls 'modes' or 'individual things' or 'finite things', which certainly fall into the category of 'things produced by God', do not exist in the way in which God does. For in the case of modes, their existence does not follow from their own nature or essence; while in the case of God, His existence does follow from His own nature or essence. In fact His essence and existence are identical (*E* I, 20).

This clearly suggests that the notion of existence as applied to God cannot be the same as the one applicable to individual things or modes. Consequently the criterion applicable in identifying individual things existing in the common order of nature cannot serve as a criterion for identification of God. It seems to me, properly speaking, there neither is nor can be a criterion for identifying God. That which is identifiable is an individual thing or a mode, and God is not an individual thing or a mode. An individual or a mode has to exist in that sense of 'exist' which makes it possible for it to be individuated as a thing that has been brought into existence by causes external to itself and which, once it exists, is a thing having certain essential properties that are constitutive of its nature. God, Spinoza wishes to point out, is a reality whose nature or essence is such that without it none of the particular finite things existing in the common order of nature could have the individuating characteristics they have. One might go so far as to say that substance or God to which Spinoza draws our attention is not the substance or God of his contemporaries;[9] nor does it have much in common with that of his predecessors in the history of philosophical thought. It would not be implausible to suggest that the meaning of the term 'existence' as applied by Spinoza to God or substance must be understood in a sense that is quite different from that of any other philosopher in the history of philosophy.

1.9

There are altogether eleven different proofs of God's existence in Spinoza's writings, excluding the ones quoted or explained in his correspondence. Since three of these eleven are given in his *Principles of Descartes' Philosophy,* and Spinoza did not accept everything that he reported about Descartes, they may be discounted from the eleven, especially since what he accepts in Descartes' proofs he tends to repeat in his own.[10]

It is commonly assumed that Spinoza had entertained some sort of ontological argument. Whether or not he did so and in what sense, if any, he accepted the ontological argument is a controversial matter which requires some consideration. It will have to be agreed that Spinoza's so-called 'proofs' are not arguments like Anselm's or Descartes's. Strictly speaking, if God is understood and defined as Spinoza does, then, as Harris rightly observes, no proof of his existence is needed, because God's existence is then the inescapable presupposition of the existence of

---

[9]Cf. E.M. Curley, *Spinoza's Metaphysics* (Harvard, 1969), Ch. I. Curley offers substantive arguments to clarify the distinctions between Spinoza's notion of substance and that of some others, e.g., Locke, Descartes, Aristotle. And I fully agree with his analysis.

[10]Cf. H.G. Hubbeling, *Spinoza's Methodology* (Netherlands, 1964), Appendix I. Hubbeling correctly refers to the following sources: three in *Short Treatise* I, three in *Ethics* I, 11; three in *Principles of Descartes' Philosophy,* I Pros. 5,6,7; one informal one in *Ethics* I, 7 and one in Scholium to *EI*, 11.

any and every thing, and the indispensable presumption of all thinking and of all truth.[11] Even the supposition of God's nonexistence would imply his existence.

Let us take the most general form of the ontological argument, namely that the necessary existence of God, as perfect being, is self-evident, for otherwise He would not be God (or perfect). It is often suggested that this sort of proof was the one that was closest to Spinoza's heart,[12] and that he was committed to it.[13] The clearest form of this argument may be taken to be the one with which the *Short Treatise* opens. Here Spinoza says, "Whatever we clearly and distinctly understand as belonging to the nature of a thing, we can also truly affirm of that thing. That existence belongs to the nature of God we can clearly and distinctly understand. Therefore [God exists]" (*ST* I).

One quick point to note here is that the 'clear and distinct understanding' of which Spinoza speaks is not to be taken as just any kind of thinking or conceiving that a human being might engage in. Indeed, it seems to be the highest form of the three kinds of knowing that Spinoza speaks of, namely, *Scientia intuitiva* (*E* II, 40S2). This clear and distinct understanding is not something that one comes to acquire through rational argument, or, for that matter, through any kind of argument.

The thrust of Anselm's and Descartes's ontological proofs seems to be that they are offered as demonstrations or arguments for the existence of God in a characteristically Judeo-Christian theology where 'God' is taken to connote a personal being, the creator and ruler of the world. The kind of existence which these

---

[11]Cf. E.E. Harris, *Salvation from Despair* (The Hague: Martinus Nijhoff, 1973), p. 39.

[12]See Harris, ibid., p. 40.

[13]See E.M. Curley, *Spinoza's Metaphysics,* p. 41.

arguments attempt to demonstrate is the one that is attributable also to finite things which are said to be created by God. The claim made is that if the things that depend for their existence on God are real, then God as their creator must have at least as much reality as the things that are created by Him. God indeed must have more reality than finite things; but in order for Him to be God, and perfect, He must be actual or must exist in the sense in which finite things do, and he must exist unlike finite things, in the sense in which only that which is *causa sui,* but nothing else, can exist. Therefore, the ontological argument seems to be concerned, preeminently, in demonstrating the actuality of God in the sense of actuality ascribed to things in the real world of spatio-temporal dimension and scientific discourse.

Although much of the language that Spinoza uses in presenting his philosophy is taken from the Western religious and philosophical tradition, the overall direction of his thought appears to be quite different from, if not completely antithetical to, that tradition.[14] Spinoza appears to be identifying the ultimate reality which philosophical thought leads him to affirm with the God of true religion.[15] In addition, Spinoza's critique of the tendency to conceive God anthropomorphically[16] clearly suggest that he does not take God to have a personality. So the reference to 'God', as Spinoza understands it, has little, if anything, to do with the theologically conceived God. In fact, Spinoza seems to suggest that if a God such as that conceived in Judeo-Christian theology were to exist, He would not be truly God but would in-

[14]Cf. Henry E. Allison, *Benedict De Spinoza (Boston: G.K. Hall, 1975),* p. 47.

[15]Cf. T.M. Forsyth, "Spinoza's Doctrine of God in Relation to His Conception of Casuality" in *Studies in Spinoza,* ed. S. Paul Kashap (Berkeley: *University of California,* 1972), p.6.

[16]Cf. *EI8S2*; *Ep* 21,44.

stead be finite and imperfect. The only correct characterization of God's reality would then be that, to the extent that He must exist in the sense in which finite things do, God must be finite; to the extent that God must be *causa sui,* and not depend for His being on anything other than his own nature, He must be infinite. So God would not be the reality to which the term 'absolutely infinite' could apply. The only term correctly applicable to Him would be that God is 'infinitely finite', with one foot, so to say, in the finite world and the other in the infinite. This may appear to some to be an attractive way of looking at things. Certainly Spinoza would look upon the notion of 'infinite finitude' applied to God as contradictory to the nature of God.

It seems, therefore, that to apply the term 'ontological proof' to Spinoza's insight into the nature of the reality to which he applied the term 'God', is not only to misunderstand the character of his assertions, but also to misunderstand the nature of his God. This misconception involved in reducing Spinoza's insight to the mold of ontological argument is a consequence, I think, of the failure to take account of the distinction that Spinoza makes between the two kinds of existence referred to earlier. One is to conceive of things as actual or existing with relation to, as he says, "a definite time and place", and the other is to conceive of them "under the form of eternity" or as eternal. Conceiving an idea to be eternally true is a consequence of the eternal nature of the thing of which an eternally true idea is an idea. That which is clearly and distinctly understood as belonging to the nature of a thing can also be asserted or affirmed with truth. Because the necessary and essential nature of a thing is clearly understood (this, I take it, is necessity *de re)* this understanding can also be expressed with statements in the form of assertions that are necessarily true (this, I take it, is necessity *de dicto).* Spinoza seems to be saying that the only way one can give true expression to the nature of reality that is God is by means of expressions that cannot be denied without involving self-contradiction. Contrary to the generally accepted view that all statements claimed to be necessarily or analytically true are empty of content, Spinoza appears to maintain that not all such statements are contentless. If the nature of reality can be accurately expressed only in terms of statements whose denial involves a contradiction, then to take such statements to be about nothing is to fail to understand the nature of the thing they are supposed to concern. They can be uninformative only so long as one attends merely to the forms of language (i.e., grammar, syntax, semantics) through which it is expressed without understanding the character of the thing or the object that is being referred to. This is quite a radical view, but Spinoza's insight may well be correct.

To say that God is eternal is to say that God's being or reality is a consequence of his very nature. And God is the *only* reality whose very essence is to be actual. This sense of 'actual' is, clearly, not the sense in which those things that are said to follow from his nature are actual or exist. Individual things, modes or modal realities, since they depend for their existence on things other than themselves, are not the kind of things whose existence 'follows from their essence'. Hence no individual thing or mode can ever be actual in the sense in which God is actual. Unfortunately, the impression that has influenced our imagination and our language is that God must be actual or exist at least in the sense in which modes are actual or exist. The force of Spinoza's insight seems to be quite the opposite. He appears to be saying that the sense in which God is actual is not the sense in which anything else is actual, except perhaps the whole system of modal manifestation. Even the whole system of modal existence, however, is said to follow from the eternal nature of God (*E* I,

16), whereas God's reality does not need to be explained by reference to anything other than *His own nature.*

This is what is meant by saying that God is the 'free cause' (*E* I, 17C2). Even the actuality of '*natura naturata*' (which Spinoza takes to *follow* from God as a free cause [*E* I, 29S]), as a single modal manifestation of God's essence, falls short of being identical with the actuality of God. It is more than obvious that the sense in which existence is applicable to God is very different from the sense in which existence is applicable to nature as a system of modes. But the precise sense in which God is actual or exists does not seem to be one that can be made intelligible by any argument. All that can be made intelligible is the sense in which God does not exist; but the sense in which he does exist remains, ultimately, to be a matter grasped through *scientia intuitiva* and not something amenable to 'reasoning' or 'proof' or 'argument' in any of the generally accepted senses of these terms.[17]

---

[17]Martha Kneale's contention that the notions 'eternity' and 'sempiternity' are either identical or the two notions entail each other [see "Eternity and Sempiternity," *Proceedings of the Aristotelian Society,* 69 (1968-69), pp. 223-238. Reprinted in *Spinoza, A Collection of Critical Essays (Doubleday, Anchor, 1973),* edited by Marjorie Grene, pp. 227-240] seems to me to betray the concern with temporal existence which was of importance to proponents of ontological argument such as Descartes and Anselm. They wished to establish the actuality of God in the sense in which things exist in 'the real world'. Kneale states, "I would go so far as to say that it is true. . . . that if God exists, he has existed a day longer today than he had existed yesterday." Of course the point she is making is about the logical relation between the two notions; but if the kind of things about which it mades sense to speak of as lasting in time, or having duration, must be capable of being individuated and hence be finite modes, then to speak of God in terms that are applicable to finite individual things would be to reduce God to the level of things that are said to be created by Him. Mrs. Kneale rightly observes that there is one way of taking Spinoza's remark in *E* I, 33S2 that there is in eternity neither when, before, nor after "which makes it quite true and harmless," if it means that there is no sense in

Spinoza observes, "In nature there is nothing contingent, but all things are determined from the necessity of the divine nature to exist in a certain manner", and "Whatever is, is in God; but God cannot be called a contingent thing, for he exists necessarily and not contingently" (*E* I, 29 and D). We must understand him to mean here that in the common order of nature there is nothing for which, in principle, there can be no explanation in terms of causes and reasons that are independent of the thing to be explained. Since substance or God is not an individual thing in the common order of nature, His existence cannot be explained by reference to the kind of conditions that are relevant in explaining the existence of things in the common order of nature. This is clearly consistent with the logical distinction Spinoza makes between the kinds of existence attributable to modes and to God or substance. He might as well have said, to use Kierkegaard's phrase, "God does not exist, He creates."

Spinoza states further that" all things are determined from a necessity of the divine nature, not only to exist, but to exist and act in a certain manner. . . . " (*E* I, 29D). He must be understood to mean that every fact in the universe is, in principle, explainable by reference to the conditions without which it would not be a fact of its kind.

---

asking of an eternal object such as God when he began to exist or when he will cease to exist. Since there wasn't a time when he did not exist he is not in time. But this is not to say, she claims, "that he does not exist at any time, i.e., not yesterday, today or tomorrow." Mrs. Kneale fails to see that if an object is not the *kind* of object to which any temporal qualifications can be applicable, then to insist on claiming that temporal qualifications must yet be truly applcable to it would not only be self-contradictory but would amount to a failure to understand the nature of the object under consideration. Mrs. Kneale seems to be confusing the nontemporal 'never' or 'always' with the temporal never and always.

1.10

In Spinoza's writings, the phrases: 'essence of God', 'power of God', 'nature of God', 'definition of God', 'the perfection of God', 'the necessity of the divine nature', 'the laws of the divine nature', 'intellect of God', 'will of God', and 'idea of God', are all equivalent in reference, though different in their sense.

The inclusion of intellect of God, will of God, and idea of God in the above list requires some justification. Spinoza appears to differentiate what he calls 'infinite intellect' from God's intellect and idea of God (*idea Dei*). I believe this distinction is necessary in order to avoid further confusion about the nature of reality referred to by the term 'God'. In *E* I, 31, for instance, he states "The actual intellect, whether it be finite or infinite, together with will . . . must be referred to the *natura naturata* and not to the *natura naturans.*" In speaking of God's intellect, however, he points out that "His intellect and His will are not distinguishable from his essence" (*E* I, 33S2). Now, since the term *natura naturans* refers to "That which is in itself and is conceived through itself, or the attributes of substance which express eternal and infinite essence, that is to say, God insofar as He is considered as a free cause" (*E* I, 29S), and *natura naturata* refers to "Everything which *follows* from the necessity of the nature of God, or of any one of God's attributes, that is to say, all the *modes* of God's attributes . . . which without God can neither be nor can be conceived" (*E* I, 29S, my emphasis), then whatever comprises the essence of God will surely belong to *natura naturans* and not to *natura naturata.* God's intellect, therefore, which is taken by Spinoza to be indistinguishable from (i.e., identical with) His essence, must belong to *natura naturans,* and not to *natura naturata.* Both the finite and infinite intellect belong to the latter as modes that depend for their being or reality upon the necessity of the divine nature which is *causa sui* or a 'free cause' of its own being or reality.

Also, in *E* I, 16 Spinoza states "From the necessity of the divine nature infinite numbers of things in infinite ways . . . must follow." And towards the end of the Scholium to *E* I, 15, he states that "everything which takes place takes place . . . from the necessity of His essence." Then in *E* II, 4 he speaks of 'The idea of God' *(Idea Dei)* from which "infinite numbers of things follow in infinite ways. . . . " It seems that Spinoza identifies the idea of God, in some sense, as he does God's intellect with the necessity of the Divine nature, or (which is the same thing) with the necessity of His essence. The question, then, is whether Spinoza makes a distinction between the infinite intellect (which as a mode is referred to *natura naturata)*, and God's intellect or the idea of God (which, being identical with God's essence, must be referred to *natura naturans)*. It seems to me that, in light of Spinoza's distinction between the two kinds of actuality or existence, the kind which can be ascribed to things belonging to *natura naturata* must be different from the kind ascribed to what falls under *natura naturans.* Accordingly, the infinite intellect, as a mode, and therefore belonging to *natura naturata,* cannot be the same as God's intellect which, as His essence, must be referred to *natura naturans.* It would also follow that God's intellect and the idea of God cannot exist or be actual in the sense in which to be actual is to exist as part of *natura naturata.* This is perhaps a minor point, but it is well to set the record straight.

1.11

Spinoza's phrase *Deus sive Natura* (God or Nature) has been understood by some to suggest that God, for Spinoza, is identical with Nature in the sense of the universe as a whole[18] (i.e., the physical world governed by natural laws which is the object of scientific investigation and scientific knowledge, or, in other words, the phenomenal world given to sense experience). Such an interpretation appears to be a consequence of a failure to take into account the distinction between the kind of existence ascribed to that which belongs to *natura naturans* and that which belongs to *natura naturata.* Some have suggested that, for Spinoza, *natura naturans* is identical with *natuat naturata,*[19] and in that sense God and Nature are the same. It has also been suggested that God is identical with the 'totality of the real',[20] thereby asserting that God subsumes *natura naturans* and *natura naturata.*

None of these views seem to me to have unquestionable support in Spinoza's writing. What Spinoza undeniably holds is that God, as *causa sui,* is an independent reality which needs nothing other than its own nature to exist in the sense of being eternal. But *natura naturata,* which follows as a consequence of this nature of God, is not and cannot be said to be itself *causa sui,* as though it did not need anything other than its own nature to exist. This point is clarified in unmistakable terms in the *Short Treatise* (1.8). Here Spinoza speaks of dividing the whole of nature, the totality of the real, into *natura naturans*—that is, as being

---

[18]Cf. S. Hampshire, *Spinoza* (Harmondsworth: Penguin, 1951), pp. 34ff.

[19]Cf. Arne Naess, "Environmental Ethics and Spinoza's Ethics," *Inquiry,* Vol. 23, No. 3, 1980, p. 322. See also *Freedom, Emotion and Self-subsistence* (Oslo: Universitetsforlaget, 1975), pp. 62–63. Professor Naess' observations in these two pages on the notion of 'God's immanence' are illuminating. I am in agreement with him for the most part, although I fail to see how accepting that Spinoza's substance *is* in itself but *exists* through or in the modes entails that Spinoza's *natura naturans* is identical with *natura naturata.*

[20]Cf. Harris, *Salvation from Despair,* p. 48.

conceived clearly and distinctly through itself, without the need of anything else (all the attributes of God, that is substance or God) and *natura naturata,* or the modes of substance, both infinite and finite, which depend on God and require substance in order to be understood. This being the case, the term substance or God in Spinoza cannot refer to the universe as a whole or to nature as the totality of the real, or to *natura naturata,* but only to its active or creative part, 'the source and origin of nature', 'the primary elements of nature', or 'the first principles of nature' of which he speaks in *DIE* 75. This clearly makes God, as *natura naturans,* the origin and source, to be, as Curley rightly observes, "something 'less than the totality of things'."[21]

Furthermore, if God were to be identical with nature as the whole system of modes, then it is difficult to see why Spinoza takes such pains to distinguish between *natura naturans* and *natura naturata.* If God and modes, between them, exhaust everything that can exist, and if God or His essence is identical with the system of modes, then what is it that keeps Spinoza from stating simply and clearly that there is no difference between the whole system of modes and God? Yet there is not a single place in his entire writings, that I can see, where he says this. The reason for this seems to be that it would be patently false to identify God or all His attributes (*Deus sive omnia Dei attributa*) (*E* I, 19) with the system of modes without endowing the modal system itself with a self-creative power thereby making the reality of God wholly superfluous. This would not be acceptable to Spinoza. *Natura naturans,* Spinoza wishes to point out, is indeed inseparable from *natura naturata,*[22] but that does not mean that for him they are identical.

---

[21]Cf. Curley, *Spinoza's Metaphysics,* p. 42.

[22]Cf. *Ep* 6. Spinoza says in this letter that he "could not *separate* God from Nature" (my italics).

1.12

When Spinoza says "All things are in God," and "Whatever is, is in God, and nothing can either be, or be conceived, without God" (*E* I, 15 and S), a question arises about the sense of 'in' that is involved here. If God is understood to be identical with the universe or nature conceived as a whole, the word 'in' may be understood as 'contained in'. This would be highly misleading, however, for the universe or nature conceived as a whole or the totality of the real, would have to include both *natura naturata* and *natura naturans.* We have seen that Spinoza appears to reserve the term 'God' for *natura naturans* alone. Hence the meaning of 'in' as it occurs in these statements needs to be understood not in terms of the spatial metaphor 'containing', but by reference to the phrase 'nothing can be or be conceived without God'. That is to say, the existence of a thing cannot be fully understood without understanding the answer to the question 'why is it what it is?' or 'what is it that brings it about?' And the only adequate answer to these questions must take the form of an explanation which is at once complete and also the ultimate explanation of its existence.

For Spinoza, the terms 'substance', 'God' and 'nature' refer precisely to such an explanatory prinicple. "Nature," he writes, "is known through itself, and not through any other thing" (*ST* App. 1 Cor.; also *ST* I, Second Dialogue). To know a thing, in other words, is to know the conditions of its existence. To understand and give expression to such conditions is to explain why that thing is what it is. Since the ultimate principle of explanation of all things cannot be explained by reference to anything but itself (*DIE* 92 and footnote, and *ST* I, 5), to ask for an explanation of the very conditions which make an explanation complete is to ask an unintelligible question, for there can be no answer to it.

This is expressed by Spinoza in the statement, "Nature is known through itself, and not through any other thing."

1.13

Spinoza not only states that "All things . . . are in God," but he also adds "Everything which takes place takes place by the laws . . . of the infinite nature of God . . . " (*E* I, 15S). This is the first time that the word 'law' is used in the *Ethics*. Later it occurs several times in different phrases. For instance, Spinoza speaks of "the law of the divine nature" from which infinite numbers of things are said to follow in infinite ways (*E* I, 17D). One is inclined to ask whether Spinoza uses the term 'laws' in these contexts in the sense in which we ordinarily use it to speak of 'scientific laws'. This is a rather difficult issue. The difficulty arises due to a lack of clearly formulated criteria for determining something that counts as a scientific law. There is, in fact, a threefold question here. First, one may ask what it is that makes or renders anything a law. This, in itself, is an ambiguous question. If we were to rephrase the question in terms of Spinoza's notion of 'definition', then we may ask, "What is the definition of 'law'?" Here it should be noted that the term 'law' refers to some *thing,* or reality, and is concerned with the nature of that reality, not the meaning of the word 'law'. The two questions, namely, that which addresses the meaning of the word, and that which addresses the nature of the thing the word stands for, are logically distinct questions, not to be confused with each other. The second of our threefold question is what makes a law scientific, and therefore distinct from any other kinds of laws? And third, is Spinoza's notion of 'laws of divine nature' the same as the notion of 'scientific laws', taken as descriptions of certain regularities in the physical world?

I shall not attempt to deal with these questions in isolation from one another, nor does it seem to be necessary for our purposes. If we attend to certain general features of what are ordinarily taken to be scientific laws and compare or contrast them with certain general features of what Spinoza takes to be universal laws, then it should become clear as to whether the denotation of these two expressions is the same or different. In so doing, we will leave aside the question of what exactly is the correct descriptive account of their denotation, granting that they have one. What concerns us here, in other words, is whether there is a connection between substance or God and what Spinoza calls the universal laws of nature. If we understand a scientific law to be one that is expressed in a general statement of the principles in accordance with which certain occurrences are confirmed to take place in the physical world, then we seem to be assuming that scientific laws are confined to explaining things that are part of nature, where 'nature' stands for the physical world. Spinoza's universal laws, however, (which he also calls 'laws of nature') do not seem to be confined to nature taken in the sense of the 'physical world'. He does say, for instance, that nothing happens in nature in contravention of its universal laws (*TPT* VI). He also points out that by 'nature' he does not mean merely matter and its modifications, but infinite other things besides matter. Again, that Spinoza's God is not 'nature' taken in the sense of physical universe alone, is clear from his letter to Oldenburg (*Ep* 73) in which he says that those who think that he identifies God and Nature, where by 'nature' is meant a certain mass or corporeal matter, "are entirely mistaken."

The universal laws of which Spinoza speaks are declared by him to be immutable and fixed. There is no doubt that these immutable universal laws are no other than what he calls 'the laws of the divine nature' or 'the necessity of the divine nature', from which infinite things in infinite ways are said to follow (*E* I, 16 and 17D). These laws are identical with God's power or God's essence. It is God's power, essence, or nature alone, that can be said to be immutable, since change and mutability involve duration, whereas the essence or nature of God can only be understood as timeless or eternal.

"The term 'law' taken absolutely," Spinoza observes, "signifies that according to which each individual, or all or some members of the same species, act in one and the same fixed and definite manner" (*TPT* IV). This statement does give some justification for understanding his universal laws as identical to what we call scientific laws, which are formulated to explain events that occur in the physical universe. But since he maintains that by 'Nature' he does not mean merely matter and its modifications but infinite other things besides matter, it would seem to be misleading, if not a mistake, to identify his universal laws with our scientific laws which are concerned almost exclusively with explaining events that are physical phenomena.

The laws that are formulated in the positive sciences take the form of hypotheses by the very nature of scientfic investigation; these are more or less confirmed or confirmable, and capable of being modified in the light of new data. This is the sense involved in saying that statements of scientific law are not logically necessary. In other words, they are not immutable or eternally true in the way that Spinoza holds univesal laws to be immutable.

Spinoza's contention that everything which occurs in nature is determined by universal laws should not be understood to be based upon belief in the law of causality in a narrow sense. That is to say, his principle of causality cannot be adequately expressed by saying that what takes place at a certain point and time depends entirely upon what has been happening in the immediate neighborhood just before. His notion of 'universal laws', while it includes this sense of causality, includes much more as well. His universal laws, it seems, would still be immutable even if the so-called 'constants of nature' (such as the constant of gravitation), and with them the formulations of the laws of nature which we accept today, did not remain absolutely constant but were to change, for instance, with the age of the astronomical universe. Spinoza would maintain that the change in the constancy of gravitation itself occurs in accordance with universal laws, even if we can never discover what they are. "Nature," Spinoza states, "always observes laws and rules, which involve eternal necessity . . . although they may not all be known to us. . . . " (*TPT* VI). Therefore, to identify Spinoza's universal laws with scientific laws, which are no more than mutable descriptions of the structure of reality formulated by human minds, would be to fail to understand the nature of reality that he calls 'God'.

The logical distinction between scientific laws and Spinoza's universal laws or laws of divine nature may be further clarified as follows: Those laws which are formulated by the human mind as a result of observation of certain spatio-temporal occurrences in order to explain some physical phenomena, and laws whose pervasive presence is the condition for the possibility of such a formulation, are not one and the same. The first kind are, strictly speaking, inductions which may conceivably be otherwise. To speak of laws in the latter sense, however, is to refer to that feature of reality in the absence of which the spatio-temporal occurrences that provide the basis for our recognition of certain regularities in nature would fail to occur. Spinoza's universal laws seem to be of the second kind rather than the first. He appears to allude to this distinction in the Second Dialogue of the *Short Treatise* when he says, "Of the necessary things which are required to bring a thing into existence some are there in order that they should produce the thing, and others in order that the thing should be capable of being produced." Thus the universal laws to which Spinoza refers may indeed be said to operate in the spatio-temporal scheme, and hence exist, insofar as the common order of nature is itself definable by reference to them; but they cannot logically be said to exist in the sense in which events or occurrences which manifest these laws do. This is all the more reason why Spinoza should hold his universal laws to be fixed, immutable, and eternal. It is this character of such laws that Spinoza expresses by saying "God is eternal, or all His attributes are eternal" (*E* I, 19), and "the existence of God . . . is an eternal truth" (*E* I, 19S).

As to how one should understand Spinoza's conception of substance, the question may still be asked, what does it mean to say that substance is "that which is in itself and is conceived through itself"? It seems that, in light of the examination and analysis in the foregoing pages, the only possible answer would be that 'substance' refers to that reality which depends upon nothing else for the nature it has; that is, it is 'in itself'. Its nature can only be understood by reference to itself, and hence it is self-explanatory or conceived through itself. To ask 'why is it what it is?' or 'why is it at all?' and to expect an answer in the form of a description of conditions which explain its being what it is, is to misconceive the character of the reality referred to in the statement of the definition. Substance, or God, Spinoza appears to say, is that primal principle, force, energy, or reality, which is the ultimate and original condition for the complete explanation of whatever is the case in the universe.

1.14

What Spinoza means by 'mode' should have become fairly clear by now. "By mode," he says, "I understand the affections of substance, or that which is in another thing through which also it is conceived" (*E* I, D5). It is evident that 'mode' is a general term he uses to refer to any member of the class of dependent things, without any specification of the way in which one mode may differ from another.

If the notion of being 'in itself' is understood to mean, as in the case of substance, that a thing depends upon nothing else for its existence and the nature it has, then it is clear that the notion of being 'in another' must be understood to mean that it depends upon something else for its existence and the nature it has. A mode is also that which is conceived through something else. This must be understood, in line with our interpretation of the notion of substance as it is conceived through itself, to mean that the explanation of a mode must logically involve a reference to something other than its own nature or character. When we ask why a particular thing is what it is, or why it is at all, we must expect an answer in the form of a description of the conditions for its explanation which includes reference to things other than itself. Any particular or individual thing of any kind whatsoever is, for Spinoza, a mode. A finite organization of modes is also to be regarded as a mode.[23] Thus a human being is a mode; so is a feeling, an emotion, a thought, or an action. The laws of thermodynamics as understood by the human mind is a mode, as it is when operating in the universe independently of human thought. Any explanation of a mode, in order to be complete, will necessarily involve reference not only to other modes but also to that ultimate principle, namely, God, which is the original cause but not itself an effect, and without which no individual thing or a mode can ever be fully explained or understood.

1.15

God is also understood by Spinoza to be a "substance consisting

---

[23]Cf. *E*IID7.

of infinite attributes" (*E* I, D6). He explains, "By attribute, I understand that which the intellect perceives of substance as constituting its essence" (*E* I, D4). One thing that is important to keep in mind is that the 'attributes' that Spinoza speaks of are not to be confused with 'properties' or 'qualities'. He makes it quite clear in the *Short Treatise* (I.2.) that by 'attributes' he means what "might be called *proper attributes* of God [i.e., which may truly be called God's attributes] through which we come to know him [as he is] in himself, and not [merely] as he acts [towards things] outside himself." In the same paragraph and elsewhere[24] he says that the attributes of God that "are known to us consist of two only, namely, *Thought and Extension.*" He also warns us that "All else . . . that men ascribe to God beyond these two attributes," such as the fact that He exists through Himself, is eternal, immutable, and so forth, are "extraneous denominations." Also, things ascribed to God that refer to his activity, such as that he is the first cause . . . etc., "all these are *properties* of God" but they are not what he calls 'attributes' of God; for the properties give us no idea as to what God is, or of what he is constituted, or what his nature is.

Now, of course, if the attributes are said to be what the intellect perceives as constituting God's essence, and God consists of infinite attributes, then logically the intellect that is able to perceive all the attributes of God will have to be the infinite intellect and not a finite one. Nevertheless, and this is an important point, since Spinoza does say clearly that *we*, meaning human beings endowed with finite intellects, "have so far not been able

[24]Cf. *ST* I, 1. Towards the end of the long footnote he states "we have so far not been able to discover more than two attributes" which belong to God. And in *ST* I, 7, in the first footnote, while speaking of "the attributes of which God consists" he says, "It is true . . . that up to the present only two of all these infinites are known to us. . . . " See also EII A5.

to discover more than two attributes" (*ST* I, 1 Footnote), and also that "there is nothing more evident to us than the fact that every entity is conceived by us under some attribute" (*Ep* 9), then it makes sense to ask what exactly would fit the reference of attributes available through human perception.[25]

If we ask, therefore, what it is that human beings perceive when they perceive something, the only correct answer would be that either they perceive or experience things existing in the world as extended objects, such as mountains, rivers, trees, and other bodies, or they perceive and experience a nonextended world of ideas, desires, feelings, emotions, dreams, and sensations. It is quite obvious that all objects of human perception or experience fall into one or the other of these two classes; they are either objects (i.e., modes of Extention), or very generally speaking, nonextended thought objects (i.e., modes of Thought). Neither of these two classes of objects is less real or actual than the other. The book that I see in front of me is as real as the *feeling* of fatigue from writing that I experience in my hands. There is an important difference, however, in that the feeling I experience is not itself an extended object, even though it is related to one.

---

[25]Francis Haserot's discussion of this point (cf. "Spinoza's Definition of Attribute" in *Studies in Spinoza, ed. Kashap, pp. 28-42)* is illuminating, but it seems to me to lose sight of the following crucial point. Spinoza uses the term 'attribute' for the reason (which he states clearly in *Ep* 9) that it is through out intellect that we perceive and *attribute,* i.e., ascribe, this or that nature to substance, even though substance is equivalent to the attributes. I shall have more to say on this point later. However, to discuss whether it is the 'infinite' or the 'finite' intellect Spinoza is referring to is in a sense quite beside the point and rather misleading. The significant point to note is that whatever it is that we *percieve* through our intellect as constituting, and which in *fact* constitutes, the nature of the primary principle or substance is what Spinoza understands by an attribute. And since Spinoza often says that the finite intellect *has* an adequate idea of God, he must be understood to mean that it apprehends the nature of God adequately through the attributes it perceives.

The feeling is an object of a different kind. My thoughts do not have spatial dimension even though they are connected with things such as my brain and body which do.

Now Spinoza holds that "Whatever is, is in God, and nothing can either be or be conceived without God" (*E* I, 15). It would follow, then, that both the above classes of things will have to be, for him, *in* God, and must be *conceived through* God. In other words, the whole range of objects of human experience or perception, must be explained and understood through reference to the ultimate source and origin, the primary elements, the essence or nature of God, or the question as to why human beings perceive or experience things as either extended objects or as thought objects will remain unanswerable. Thought and Extension are two categories or attributes that constitute the nature of the universe as we know it. These categories themselves are not given to sense perception or experience. What is perceived or experienced through the senses are individual modes that belong to either one or the other category.[26] It is only through the intellect, as distinct from the senses, that the categories or attributes are perceived or apprehended. The human intellect, however, has a limited range. While we actually perceive objects as belonging to only two categories, we cannot conclude that these are all or the only categories to which objects can (logically) belong. Spinoza's statement in *E* I, D6, that substance consists of infinite attributes,

[26]Cf. *Ep* 10. Simon DeVries asks whether we need experience to know whether the definition of some attribute is true. Spinoza replies that we only need experience to know the existence of modes, because their existence doesn't follow from their own nature, "but we do not need experience in the case of those things whose existence is not distinguished from their essence and therefore follows from their definition," i.e., their nature. And "since the existence of attributes does not differ from their essence we shall not be able to apprehend it by any kind of experience."

therefore, lends itself to being understood as saying that the possibility of objects belonging to categories other than the ones perceived by the human intellect is, in fact, indeterminable. This is in line with Spinoza's remarks in his letter to Boxel: "I do not say that I know God entirely, but only that I understand some of His attributes, though not all, nor even the greater part of them, and it is certain that our ignorance of the majority of them does not hinder our having knowledge of some of them" (*Ep* 56).

Spinoza's expression "God or all his attributes" (*E* I, 19) (*Deus, sive omnia Dei attributa*) clearly indicates that God is identical with all his attributes, for attributes constitute the reality that is God. There is nothing over and above all the attributes that is the reality referred to by the term 'God'. In that sense, to say that God is absolutely infinite is to say that all the attributes, taken together, exhaust all the categories to which things that can be said to be real or to exist can belong. Each attribute or category taken by itself, however, does not include any of the others. Each is complete in itself, or as Spinoza puts it, "infinite in its own kind" (*in suo genere*) (*E* I, D6). Since each excludes the others, and only all taken together constitute the ultimate principles of the existence of everything that can possibly be, then God (i.e., all attributes taken as a whole) alone can be said to be absolutely infinite. The sense of the expression 'absolutely infinite' is distinct from that of the expression 'infinite in its own kind.' The latter characterizes each single attribute. There is a sense, nevertheless, in which each attribute is limited by other attributes insofar as there are, for any attribute, others besides itself. God or all the attributes leave nothing outside themselves for them to be limited by. Spinoza expresses this notion of 'infinite in its own kind' with great clarity in a letter to Oldenburg. He points out that if we admit that Thought does not pertain to the nature of Extension, then "Extension cannot be limited by Thought

. . . . But if anyone says that Extension is not limited by Extension but by Thought, is that not the same as saying that Extension is not infinite absolutely, but only in so far as it is Extension? That is, he does not allow that Extension is infinite absolutely but only in so far as it is Extension, that is, in its own kind." (*Ep* 4).

1.16

Any particular object or mode belonging to one or the other category is completely explainable within the framework of a single category. There is no possibility of causal interdependence between the categories themselves (since they are independently real) or between objects belonging to different categories. All the known and unknown categories of explanation together constitute the principles of explanation of the nature of everything in the universe. This being the case, one can perhaps understand Spinoza's statement, "I understand by attribute all that which is conceived through itself and in itself; so that its conception does not involve the conception of some other thing" (*Ep* 2). When we compare this with his statement in *E* I, D3, "By substance, I understand that which is in itself and is conceived through itself; in other words, that, the conception of which does not need the conception of another thing from which it must be formed," the similarity is remarkable. It seems that 'attribute' is just another term for 'substance'. This could have been misleading had Spinoza not clarified this point in a letter to DeVries (*Ep* 9) in which he repeats the statement he makes in his definition of substance in *E* I, D3, and adds, "I mean the same by attribute, except that it is called attribute with respect to the intellect, which attributes such and such nature to substance." What this means, clearly, is that these attributes have nothing to do with properties or qualities, for all the attributes taken together constitute the essence of God. God is identical with the unity of all attributes. They are attributes of God, not in the sense in which God is a thing of which a quality is being predicated, but in the sense in which each attribute is one of the unity of attributes that is God. We know the nature of God in apprehending the categories which explain the nature of various objects of our experience. An attribute is what the intellect comprehends as constituting the essence of substance. Quite understandably then, all the categories of explanation taken together would be identical with the ultimate principles of the explanation of every thing. To claim this, however, is the same as to say, in Spinoza's terms, that substance or God or all his attributes are one and the same. And one attribute cannot, of course, exhaust all the explanatory principles. Each attribute, nevertheless, is substantial in character in the sense that it does not and cannot depend upon anything else for the explanation of its nature. This clearly must be the reason for the similarity in his statements about the nature of substance and attribute.

1.17

For Spinoza 'Extension', 'extended substance', 'corporeal substance', and 'infinite quantity' are all equivalent expressions. Extension as attribute is not something that is measurable. It is not itself a body composed of parts (*E* I, 15S). In speaking of corporeal substance or extended substance, Spinoza is not talking about a body in space and time, or about a quantity which we perceive through the senses. He makes the point that "Quantity is conceived by us in two ways: either abstactedly or superficially; that is to say, as we imagine it, *or else* as substance, in which way it is conceived by the intellect alone" (*E* I, 15S). To think of quantity abstactedly or superficially is what Spinoza evidently means by perceiving it through the senses. He says that it is only when quantity is imagined, or as it exists in imagination, that it can be found to be "finite, divisible and composed of parts; but if we regard it as it exists in the intellect and conceive it insofar as it is substance then . . . we find it to be infinite, one, and indivisible."

It is quite clear that Spinoza's 'extended substance' is not the phenomenal world given to sense perception. It is, as pointed out earlier, a category of explanation of the existence of things in the phenomenal world. Unlike the phenomenal objects that are given to sense experience, however, the categories are only accessible through the intellect or thought.

Similarly, the attribute 'Thought' does not stand, *qua* attribute, for any kind of mental occurrence, particular or general. It is not even a thought in God's mind, whatever that may mean. It is a category which is the necessary condition for the explanation of all the individual things we experience which are not extended objects, but are what I term, 'thought objects' or modes of Thought, and what Spinoza refers to as 'ideas'.

Furthermore, and importantly, attributes are not merely categories of explanation but also categories of existence. That is to say, it is because individual things or modes can only exist as modes of this or that *kind*, (i.e., of one or the other *attribute*) that their explanation must necessarily involve reference to the attribute or category to which they belong, or of which they are modes. This being the case, we should expect that Spinoza will have all the more reason to hold that the kind of existence ascribed to individual things or finite modes cannot be applicable to the attributes. This is precisely what he does say. In his letter to Meyer (*Ep* 12) Spinoza observes that from a consideration of the existence of finite modes we cannot conclude anything about their existence in the future. In other words, there is nothing in the nature of individual things themselves from which their existence could be said to follow, for they depend for their existence not upon their own nature but upon something external to or other than themselves. This is the reason why, although they exist, we can conceive of them as nonexistent; but, he remarks, "We conceive the existence of substance as entirely different from the existence of modes." Since there is no difference between the nature of substance and attribute, it follows that the kind of existence applicable to attributes must also be entirely different from that applicable to modes. It is from this difference, in fact, that there arises the difference between eternity and duration in Spinoza's thought.

Duration, taken in the sense of temporal existence, is applicable only to the existence of finite modes; however, Spinoza states, "We can explain the existence of Substance only by means of Eternity" (*Ep* 12). Now if one takes the notion of 'existence' exclusively in the sense which applies to spatio-temporal things that causally depend upon something external to their own nature, and the term 'necessary' to apply to that which is *causa sui,* then clearly it is no more than a truism that 'necessary existence' is a logically self-contradictory notion. The phrase 'necessary existence', however, taken in the sense to which Spinoza draws our attention by the use of the term 'eternal' in its application to God, which stands for non-spatio-temporal existence, would seem to be not merely logically possible but, indeed, logically necessary; for without the applicability of the concept of necessary existence, the notion of contingent or conditional existence will remain unexplainable. This is what he was pointing to in his response to the argument of infinite regress (*Ep* 12) alluded to earlier.

1.18

The last point that requires consideration in this chapter is Spinoza's notion of freedom as it applies to God. It is especially important because it provides an insight into the origin of Spinoza's idea of freedom.

Spinoza states "God acts from the laws of his own nature only and is compelled by no one" (*E* I, 17). By 'compelled' (*coactus*) (i.e., 'constrained' or 'forced') he can only mean what he would mean if he had said 'externally determined' or 'caused to act' in the sense in which modes are dependent upon something other than their own nature to be or to exist. Now what sense does it make to say 'God acts' or 'God is not compelled to act' if 'God' is understood in the sense in which we have interpreted it?

Suppose we take him to be saying that the ultimate source and origin, the first principle, or *natura naturans,* is, by its very nature, an active principle whose activity cannot be explained by reference to anything external to itself without its forfeiting its *causa sui* character and becoming merely the first in the infinite chain of causal series; and if it were not active by its very nature then no modal existence could have been possible since modes are not *causa sui.* Now it is possible to claim that there is a kind of circularity involved in this conception of the relation between *natura naturans* and *natura naturata.* Modal existence seems to be employed as evidence to provide the guarantee that the primary principle is an active principle, while the active character of the primary principle is accepted as the necessary prerequisite of modal existence. I am quite certain, however, that this circularity is not a vicious one. If an argument is said to involve a vicious circularity on the grounds that, although an adequate explanation of one or the other of the two sides of the circular argument *can* be given without presupposing or entailing the other, and the author deliberately refuses to make such an attempt due to certain false assumptions, then it seems to me that Spinoza's position is not viciously circular.

Spinoza is saying that it is, in principle, impossible to understand the nature of reality, or things as they truly are, without acknowledging the self-explanatory, creative, or active nature of the primary principle that is the source and origin of nature. It is logically impossible, he suggests, "that things which do not exist . . . in virtue of their own nature, are not determined to existence by something which does exist necessarily in virtue of its own nature, and which is a cause, not an effect" (*Ep* 12). The nature of this primary principle is such that its active character can be explained only by reference to the kind of thing it is. There is and can be no appeal to another more primary principle to explain its character. To say this is the same as to say that God is not determined to exist and act by anything other than or external to itself. That is, His existence and activity follow from, or can be explained by reference to, the character of His own reality. This is what Spinoza must mean when he says, "There is no cause, either external to God or within Him, which can excite Him to act except the perfection of His own nature" (*E* I, 17C1). It also follows that it makes no sense to apply the concept of 'conscious purpose' or 'end' in explaining why the source and origin is constituted the way it is, or why it is active in the manner it is. Spinoza points this out when he says "God acts from the laws of His own nature only, and is compelled by no one" (*E* I, 17).

In the long and informative scholium to *E* I, 17 Spinoza tries to remove a general misunderstanding regarding the notion of freedom as applied to God. It is sometimes believed that when we say 'God is free', we are saying that God has power *not* to bring about things which follow from His nature. This, as Spinoza points out, is a mistake; for besides the fact that it takes away perfection from God, this interpretation deprives God of His very nature or essence from which everything that exists must follow. On these grounds, he says, "We deny that God can omit to do what He does. . . . In God it would be an imperfection to omit to do what he does" (*ST* I, 4). Spinoza is well aware that some people would regard this as blasphemy and as a belittling of God, but "such an assertion," he observes, "results from a misapprehension of what constitutes *true freedom.*"

What exactly does he mean by 'true freedom'? Spinoza tells us in unmistakable terms that true freedom is by no means what people think it is, namely, the ability to do or not to do something good or evil. True freedom consists in being in no way constrained, compelled or forced to act by anything else but one's own essential nature (*ST* I, 4). It is clear that God alone can be said to be free in this sense of 'free', for He alone can ultimately be said to be active from the laws of His own nature without being compelled or constrained by anything.

The freedom ascribed or ascribable to God has nothing whatsoever to do with freedom of the will, for God, as Spinoza says, "does not act from freedom of the will" (*E* I, 32C1). Furthermore, to say 'God is truly free' or 'God is the free cause' is to say no more than the active character of the ultimate principle of explanation cannot be understood in any other way except as being self-explanatory. In answer to the question 'Why is it what it is?' no reference can possibly be made to anything other than its own essential nature. In other words, it is impossible, in principle, to answer this question other than to say simply 'That is the way it is'. This indicates that a question of this kind posed with regard to the source and origin, the primary principle or 'God', is logically altogether different from a similar question posed with regard to the nature of individual things or modes.

Chapter Two

Ideas

2.1

Spinoza defines 'idea' as "A conception of the mind which the mind forms because it is a thinking thing" (*E* II, Df. 3). Now, it would not be difficult to show that his different uses of the term are consistent with this definition, but the fact that he uses it in many different ways is apt to generate confusion if the distinctions are not kept in mind.

Consider, for instance, Spinoza's statement, "In God there necessarily exists the idea of His essence, and of all things which necessarily follow from His essence" (*E* II, 3). Here, the term 'idea' cannot be taken literally as 'conception of the mind which the mind forms because it is a thinking thing'. Spinoza's God is not a thing which thinks in the sense in which a human being is a thing which thinks. When Spinoza says "God is a thinking thing"

(*E* II, 1), it means no more than what he says in the same proposition, namely, "Thought is an attribute of God." That is to say, Thought constitutes the *essence* of God, but it is *not a property* ascribable to God. It would be senseless to expect Thought, an attribute, to form conceptions. What sense is to be made, then, of his statement in *E* II, 3? It can only mean that to say 'The essence of God consists in the attribute of thought', is the same as to say 'In God, there necessarily exists the idea of His essence'. This latter, however, must not be understood in such a way as to render God an anthropomorphic entity believed to have ideas which are conceptions of His mind. All it means is that Thought constitutes a necessary part of the nature of reality that is being referred to by the term 'substance' or 'God'.

The term 'idea' as it occurs in *E* II, 3 is to be understood, in fact, in the sense in which Spinoza uses it in *E* II, 4: "The idea of God, from which infinite numbers of things follow in infinite ways, can be one only." 'The idea of God', is here the same thing as 'the necessity of the divine nature' (*E*, I, 16), from which infinite numbers of things follow in infinite ways. As the essence of God is identical with the attributes, Spinoza wishes to specify, by the use of the word 'idea' in respect to God, reference to one of the attributes which constitute the nature of substance—namely, to Thought, and to no other.

2.2

The term 'idea' is also used to refer to that of which the idea in an individual mind is an idea; that is to say, to a particular object of thinking which is a concept or (in the terminology of the period) an objective idea, and which I prefer to call a 'thought-object'.[1]

[1]The sense of what I call 'thought-object' is very similar to, if not the

An 'idea' in this sense is independent of being thought *of* by any finite individual mind. This is the sense in which the word 'idea' occurs in, for example, *E* II, 49 Dem., where Spinoza says that when the mind affirms that the three angles of a triangle are equal to right angles, "this affirmation involves the concept or idea (*conceptum, sive ideam*) of the triangle . . . [w]ithout it the affirmation can not be conceived."

The distinction between ideas that are 'ideas in the human mind' and ideas that are 'thought-objects' is extremely important. For Spinoza, an idea is not merely something subjective, or an idea in an individual mind, but also something objective. An objective idea is that of which the idea in any finite mind is an idea. That is to say, it is the objective idea that is the *object* of the ideation by an individual mind. This may seem a little obscure, but it is not really incomprehensible. When a person is engaged in thinking, there is necessarily something that he is thinking *about;* the activity of thinking is indeed inseparable from the object of thought, but the activity is logically distinct from the object of thinking. What we think of is an object of thought in a rather special sense. Normally we may say, "I am thinking of so and so", when 'so and so' is, for example, a person or some spatio-temporal entity. Spinoza wants to say that this can be misleading; for, when I think of a person, what I think of is the *idea* of a person; it is not the physical entity directly that is the object of thought. The object of thought is something thinkable. It is a mode of Thought, and hence a 'thought-object' which does not

---

same as, what Frege calls 'Thought' (cf. *Logical Investigations* by Gottlob Frege, ed., P.T. Geach [New Haven: Yale University Press, 1977], pp. 1–30). All future references to Frege in the course of this essay will be to the page numbers of this edition.

have the characteristics of a physical body, such as weight or extension.

Furthermore, contradictions cannot be thought-objects. There is no such objective idea or thought-object as a square circle, therefore a finite mind (or, for that matter, an infinite mind) can never form an idea of a square circle. It is thought-objects or objective ideas which Spinoza speaks of as "ideas related to God." One can see why he should say, "All ideas, in so far as they are related to God, are true" (*E* II, 32).

If I say that I am thinking (or trying to think) of a Euclidean triangle whose internal angles are not equal to two right angles, there is certainly something that I may be said to be thinking of, and whatever constitutes my idea is a mode of Thought. It is also clear that the idea in my mind, whatever else it may be, cannot be the idea of a Euclidean triangle as a thought-object. Hence, the idea in my mind is bound to be inadequate. Spinoza expresses this in his terms by saying: "When we say that God has this or that idea, not merely insofar as He forms the nature of the human mind, but insofar as He has at the same time with the human mind an idea also of another thing, then we say that the human mind perceives the thing partially or inadequately" (*E* II, 11, C).

A true idea in a human mind, being the idea of the objective idea or thought-object (i.e., idea related to God) is a manifesta tion of the nature of God through the nature of the human mind. It is such thought-objects again, that Spinoza appears to speak of when he says, "The knowledge of everything which happens in *the object of any idea* necessarily exists in God in so far as He is considered as affected with the *idea* of that object" (*E* II, 12 Dem., my italics).

Spinoza's use of the term 'knowledge' here may be somewhat puzzling. The word 'knowledge', when used with reference to God, is not to be, and cannot be construed, in the sense in which it is used with reference to human beings. Why then did Spinoza use it? What is the analogy between the two, if any, which might explain Spinoza's use of 'knowledge' with reference to God? This is not an easy question, but one plausible answer may be as follows. When I say that I have or possess a true idea, this is the same as saying that a true idea is in my mind, or that the knowledge of this idea exists in me. A true idea in my mind must be the idea of the thought-object, which is related to God insofar as the thought-object itself—as an 'idea'—is a mode of the attribute of Thought. Since saying that 'a true idea is in my mind' is the same thing as saying that the '*knowledge* of that idea exists in me', then the thought-object which, for Spinoza, is also an idea, may, by analogy, be said to be the idea 'known' to God. However, it is important to remember that the knowledge we may thus ascribe to God is not the *idea* (i.e., consciousness) of the thought-object as it is ascribed to the human mind, but the thought-object itself. Hence, the kind of knowledge ascribable to God is logically distinct from the knowledge in the human mind. Much confusion can be avoided by keeping this distinction in mind.

A particular thought-object, Spinoza wants to point out, cannot be a mode of any other attribute than Thought. That is to say, the nature of a particular concept or thought-object cannot be explained or understood by reference to any other category except Thought. Furthermore, since the human mind, as a "thinking thing', is for Spinoza nothing but a mode of Thought, its nature can be understood or apprehended only by reference to those explanatory conditions which comprise other modes of Thought. Ultimately the mind is understood by reference to the primal reality—the attribute Thought—the category to which all ideas in the human mind as well as thought-objects must belong and which is also their origin, source, or ground.

2.3

There is a much more complex use of the word 'idea' in *E* II, 7. According to this proposition, "The order and connection of ideas is the same as the order and connection of things." This is indeed one of the most important propositions in the *Ethics,* and a correct interpretation and understanding of it can have crucial consequences for gaining an insight into Spinoza's philosophy of mind and action.

Initially, the proposition seems to point out that modes of Thought that are logically related to each other have correlative modes of Extension that are causally related to each other. The term 'idea' in this proproposition does not appear to refer to 'conceptions' of any particular mind or to ideas in any human mind, but to modes of Thought as thought-objects. Spinoza might as well have expressed the proposition by saying, 'The order and connection of modes of Thought as thought-objects is the same as the order and connection of things as modes of Extension.' But this is not enough. What he intends to suggest even further is that whether we human beings conceive the world in terms of thought-objects or in terms of interconnected modes of Extension as part of the spatio-temporal order, we shall discover, if our conception is to be true, one and the same order of explanation and sequence of things.

Take the example of a circle. It will be agreed that in order to form a true conception of a circle, one must understand why a certain figure is a circle rather than anything else. That is to say, one must have a grasp of the conditions that determine the conception one has to be the conception of a circle. It will also be agreed that if a circle exists in nature as, for example, a circle drawn on a paper, then it must embody or involve the conditions that make it a circle. The essential conditions for the existence of a circle in nature are also those which need to be comprehended in forming a conception of a circle if it is to be a true conception. These conditions are numerically identical (although qualitatively distinct). That is to say, they must exist in nature, and our thinking (ideas) must involve ideas (thought-objects) of those very conditions, in order for us to form a true idea or concept of a circle. These are not two different sets of conditions. Spinoza expresses this by saying that a mode of Extension (e.g., a circle drawn on paper) and the idea of that mode (i.e., the thought-object correlative to it), are the same thing expressed in two different ways: "The order and connection of ideas is the same as the order and connection of things" (*E* II, 7). The very conditions which would explain the existence of things in the spatio-temporal order are the conditions that will have to be incorporated in the thought-objects of those things in order for our thoughts to be true thoughts of those particular things. Therefore, to paraphrase Spinoza, whether we view the world under the attribute of extension, or under the attribute of thought, we shall discover one and the same order, one and the same connection of causal relations, one and the same set of explanatory conditions (*E* II, 7S).

Furthermore, Spinoza speaks of the relation between a circle existing in nature and the idea that is in God of an existing circle by saying that these two are one and the same thing manifested through different attributes (*E* II, 7S). Now if one takes the phrase 'idea that is in God' to refer to the thought-object or the objective idea, then one can perhaps follow what Spinoza means by the following statement:

> Whatever happens in the object of the idea constituting the human mind must be perceived by the human mind; or in other words, an idea of that thing will necessarily exist in the human

> mind. That is to say, if the object of the idea constituting the human mind be a body, nothing can happen in that body which is not perceived by the mind. (*E* II, 12)

Spinoza seems to be saying that whatever constitutes the thought-object of, for instance, a circle, must be included in the conception that I form of a circle in order for the idea of a circle in my mind to be true. Because the thought-object corresponding to the idea in my mind is the thought-object correlative to the mode of extension, namely a circle existing in nature (which is a body), it is inconceivable that there can be anything which constitutes the nature or essence of that body that is not included in my true idea of it. In other words, it is in principle impossible that the idea of a thing in my mind can be true and yet fail to reflect the connections constituting the thought-object correlated with the nature of the thing as it is.

2.4

Spinoza uses the word 'thing' *(res)* to refer to modes of Thought as well as to modes of Extension. A 'thing' for him is not necessarily a body; it can also be an idea. So he says, for instance,

> When *things* are considered as modes of thought, we must explain the order of the whole of nature or the connection of causes by the attribue of thought alone, and when *things* are considered as modes of extension the order of the whole of nature must be explained through the attribute of extension alone. (*E* II, 7S, my italics)

Suppose that I think of a circle now, in that sense of 'think' in which to think is to conceive the definition of a circle in

Spinoza's sense of 'definition'. Upon learning this, someone asks me 'why did you think of a circle at this moment?' The answer to this question is not provided if I reply, 'Because that is the way a circle appears in space'. In my reply I must refer to other ideas, or modes of Thought—such as beliefs, desires, intentions—which are related in my mind to the conception I have of a circle, in such a way that following the sequence of these ideas would explain the reasons which led me to form an idea of a circle at this moment.

Again, while investigating the nature of some phenomenon, I may comprehend an aspect of it which, let us assume, leads to a more complete understanding of its character and constitution. It will be noted that my understanding of the thing's nature consists of ideas at successive stages of development. The ideas that I entertain would be true if they comprehend the nature of the thing that I endeavor to understand. The connection between ideas in my mind, at different stages, will have to be such that unless each idea (or set of ideas) were explainable by reference to other ideas (or set of ideas) logically prior to them, the question as to why I thought what I did at any given moment, would remain unanswered. Spinoza's point seems to be that the explanation of one particular idea in an individual mind can be given only by reference to conditions which consist exclusively of ideas. The term 'ideas' as used here refers to all modes of Thought, such as desires, feelings, beliefs, perceptions, and anything else that can be referred to by a mental predicate. All ideas, as individual modes, are in principle explainable by reference to other ideas as their immediate, proximate, or sufficient condition, and the attribute of thought as their ultimate necessary condition.

Suppose the thing under investigation is a body in space and time. Now, clearly, the connections between the changes occurring in it during the course of one's observations must be explainable by reference to certain spatio-temporal conditons relative to that body, which are prior to the changes themselves, together with the attribute or category of Extension-their ultimate and necessary condition. These are the conditions without which the thing being investigated would not be a physical object, nor would the changes pertaining to it be physical modifications or events in the spatio-temporal order. Interestingly, Spinoza's view is that the kind of connection which holds between one such occurrence (or set of occurrences) and another relating to the same object, is not of the kind which holds between an idea that I form about the occurrence of an event and the idea that I form of another occurrence, namely, its effect.

Spinoza often uses the word 'cause' to refer to both the rela tion between ideas and to the relation between physical events. For instance, while speaking of individual things, or modes of an attribute, he says that any finite thing or a mode having determinate existence must be determined to exist by "another cause which is also finite and has a determinate existence; and again, this cause can not exist . . . unless [determined] by another cause which is also finite . . . and so on *ad infinitum*" (*E* I, 28).

But this must not be taken to mean, as it usually is, that Spinoza makes no distinction between the physical events; or as otherwise expressed, that he confuses causal relation with logical relation. He makes it more than clear in *E* II, 7S[2] that the nature of the *idea* of a circle, for instance, can only be perceived through another, and so on *ad infinitum:*

> When things are considered as modes of thought, we must explain the order of the whole of nature . . . or the connection of

[2]Cf. also *E* II, 9 Dem.; E II, 30 Dem.; E II, 31 Dem.; and *E* III, 2 Dem.

> causes, by the attribute of thought alone, and when things are considered as modes of extension, the order of the whole of nature must be explained through the attribute of extension alone." (*E* II, 7S)

Modes of one attribute, in other words, cannot be explained by reference to conditions that explain modes of another attribute, for there is nothing in common between the different attributes themselves for one to be explained by reference to another. As Spinoza observes, "Those things which have nothing mutually in common with one another cannot through one another be mutually understood, that is to say, the conception of the one does not involve the conception of the other" (*E* I, A5). He makes the same point in the demonstration of *E* III, 2, where he says that what determines the mind to thought is a mode of Thought and not of Extension. And the motion or rest of the body must be derived from some other body and not from a mode of Thought. It therefore seems reasonable to conclude that, for Spinoza, the relation between modes of one attribute must be of a kind that is *logically distinct* from the relation between modes of another.

Now if we say, as Spinoza does, that modes of Extension can be explained only by reference to other modes of Extension as their causal condition, and this causal condition is appropriate only to the explanation of modes of Extension, then when we speak of modes of Thought as being explainable only by reference to other modes of Thought as their causal condition; we cannot possibly be using the word 'causal' to mean, nor can Spinoza be taken to be using it to mean, the same thing in both cases. What, of course, is meant by 'causal condition', in either case, is 'explanatory condition'. When Spinoza says that the order and connection of ideas is the same as the order and connection of things, what he means, as becomes clear from a careful look at the scholium to *E* III, 2, is that the *order and concatenation* of things considered as modes of Thought, (i.e., as thought-objects) is numerically identical with the order and connection of correlative modes of Extension, but the *nature of explanation* itself is qualitatively distinct, and to that extent not identical, in both instances. The kind of conditions that are relevant to the explanation of physical events (modes of Extension) have no application to the explanation of 'ideas'. This, I think, is precisely what he tries to convey by his phrase that the explanation of 'things' is conceived "at one time under the attribute of thought, and at another under that of extension" (*E* III, 2S). There is not the slightest evidence here to suggest that Spinoza made no *qualitative* distinction between the explanation given under the attribute of Thought and the one given under that of Extension, or that he confused causal relation with logical relation. One billiard ball can hit and push another billiard ball and cause it to move, but the thought-object of a billiard ball is not the kind of thing that can hit, push, or cause the thought-obect of another billiard ball to move. Spinoza does not confuse the distinction involved in these two different kinds of relations.

2.5

The term 'idea' is also used by Spinoza to refer to what we normally describe as fictions of the mind, or imaginations, which would include dreams. These are what he calls "ideas of nonexistent individual things" (*E* II, 8). The notion of 'nonexistent individual things' would also include things that may be said to be possible and/or in the future as well as those that existed in the past.[3]

---

[3]I am indebted to Dr. Bruce Kermott for the contents of this last sen-

'Idea' is also sometimes used as "the idea of individual things actually existing" (*E* II, 9,11). In this sense 'idea' refers to (1) sense perception of objects as part of the common order of nature, (2) memories of such objects, and (3) conceptions (as distinct from perceptions) of things either as part of the common order of nature or as part of the order of intellect, without the aid of direct perception or memory of them. This last use of the word 'idea' is significant in Spinoza's works, for it is 'idea' taken in this sense that Spinoza seems to regard as adequate as well as true.

2.6

The word 'object' in phrases such as "the object of the idea" (*E*II, 12 and 13) has two senses, which are correlative but distinct. In one sense, as noted above, it means the objective idea or thought-object, which is also said to be an idea existing in God or in the infinite intellect of God. In another sense, it refers not to the mode of Thought but to the mode of Extension correlated with the thought-object. To *conceive* a thought-object is to have an idea in one's mind. But to have an idea is also at times to *perceive* the mode of Extension or a body of which the objective idea is an idea.

Suppose a primitive man or a child looks at a figure of a circle drawn on paper, but does not know the conditions that ex-

---

tence. Kermott pointed out that ideas of things that do not yet exist are not the same as ideas of things that do. Nor is an idea of a thing that once existed but does not any longer the same as the idea of a thing that is still existent. An idea of a person who is alive is one thing; an idea of him when he is no longer alive, quite another. Although both may be described as 'rememberings', to confuse one with the other would lead to false knowledge. Spinoza's examples of Peter and Paul (see 2.12) would appear to suggest this distincton.

plain its nature. That is to say, he does not know, in Spinoza's terms, the 'definition' of a circle. Assuming normal eyesight, he would see the figure of a circle as would another man who understands the nature or definition of a circle. Here the visual object in both cases is the same, but the conceptual object differs. In both cases, however, the sense perception of the circle consists of the ideas (of sense perception) of the way in whch their eyes and brains are affected by an object in space and time (the circle drawn on paper). Spinoza's view seems to be that the objective idea or thought-object of the circle, as it is in nature, remains unchanged. The thought-object is, in a sense, nothing but that which can be (although in fact may not be) an object of an idea in an individual mind. When an individual mind does conceive this object, his idea of a circle is a true idea, or in other words, he understands the nature or definition of a circle.

A person may, of course, have a false idea of the circle. A false idea is one which is not the idea of the thought-object correlated with the actual circle, but the idea of a thought-object correlated with the circle as it is merely perceived by the senses, or the circle as it exists in 'imagination', as Spinoza would say. A false idea, being the idea of a thought-object of a superficial aspect of the circle, would fail to be the idea of the thought-object correlated with the circle as it is. A false idea therefore, is an inadequate idea in that it fails to be the idea of the thought-object of a thing as it is in its nature. This is what Spinoza tries to convey when he says, "Falsity consists in the privation of knowledge which inadequate ideas involve" (*E* II, 35). To be in error is not the same thing, to Spinoza, as to be ignorant. For in the case of ignorance, there clearly can be no idea involved whatsoever. The primitive man, in our example, does not suffer from absolute ignorance, for he does *perceive* the circle; but he does not *conceive* the thought-object correlated with the nature of the circle. Spinoza might want to add that what primitive man fails to conceive is not something that depends upon *his* nature for its existence. Even if there were no human beings or any sentient beings to form an idea of the thought-object correlated with a circle existing in nature, it would still remain a mode of Thought, that is, some thing conceivable in itself—"an idea in God's mind."

2.7

For Spinoza, man's knowledge of the world is confined to the ideas of the affections or modifications by which his own body is affected. The greater the complexity of the ways in which a man's body is affected by external bodies, the greater the aptitude of the human mind to perceive objects in the phenomenal world through the conception of their correlative thought-objects. The aptitude of the human mind to perceive, or have ideas, increases in proportion to the number of ways in which the body can be affected (*E* II, 14).

The human mind is composed of ideas. These ideas are initially derived from the numerous ways in which a man's body is affected by external bodies. The beginning of the formation of a human mind consists in the perception of individual things existing as objects in the spatio-temporal order. As Spinoza puts it, "The first thing which forms the actual Being of the human mind is nothing else than the idea of an individual thing actually existing" (*E* II, 11); and "The object of the idea constituting the human mind is a body, or a certain mode of Extension actually existing, and nothing else" (*E* II, 13). Thus all human knowledge, as far as human knowledge consists of ideas, begins, for Spinoza, with sense perception. All ideas, and hence all knowledge, is not, of course, confined to ideas derived from sense perception. Spinoza's view is that whether ideas in one's mind are ideas of sense perception (that is to say, the consciousness of things in the external world), or whether they are ideas of ideas, that is, ideas of reflection, there are necessarily physical changes occurring in one's body correlative to them. It is, in principle, impossible for a man to be conscious of anything, to have ideas in any sense, without correlative physical modifications occurring in his body. The changes occurring in the body, or 'affections' of the body, are modes of Extension, and their correlative thought-objects are modes of Thought or ideas. To be conscious of these modes of Thought is for an individual to have a mind or have ideas. The order and connection between ideas considered as thought-objects is, in one sense, identical with the order and connection between the sequence of physical changes occurring in the body. So when Spinoza says, "The human mind is the idea . . . of the human body" (*E* II, 19 Dem.), what he means is that those 'ideas' which are the objects of my mind, are numerically identical with the correlative modifications in my body; but the two are qualitatively distinct.

The notion of numerical identity which also involves qualitative distinction may seem, on the face of it, rather odd. I do not believe, however, that it is unintelligible or incomprehensible. The particular book in front of me, for instance, has certain physical characteristics, such as weight, color and shape; and it also contains words which express ideas. I can say that there are such and such ideas expressed in this book. I can also say that this book has a brownish jacket designed by so and so, contains so many pages, and weighs so many ounces. Both descriptions are descriptions of numerically one and the same thing; what they describe, however, are two different aspects of it. One is the physical aspect of the book, the other the nonphysical.

Spinoza could mean that all modifications of one's body

necessarily have correlative thought-objects. It is because there are these thought-objects of bodily changes that a human mind can have ideas of the changes occurring in the human body. The numerically same individual thing is being described from two qualitatively distinct points of view. Just as one cannot meaningfully explain the nature of ideas contained in the book by referring to its physical apsects, nor explain the nature of the book's physical aspects by referring to the ideas contained in it, similarly, ideas as modes of Thought cannot be explained by reference to physical changes in the body which are modes of Extension. They each require different kinds of explanations. The changes occurring in the body (as modes of Extension) and the correlative thought-objects (as modes of Thought) both refer to one and the same individual considered in terms of two distinct categories that are perceived by the intellect to constitute the nature of the ultimate force or principle in the universe.

Ideas can be explained only by reference to other ideas that are logically connected with them, and physical changes in the body can be explained only by reference to other physical changes in or outside the body that are causally connected with them. To say, as Spinoza does, "Man is composed of mind and body" (*E* II, 13C), is to imply that a human being, or a person is describable in terms of both mental and physical predicates. But to describe a person in terms of one category of predicates is not qualitatively identical with the description of him in terms of the other; yet the description in terms of each of the two categories is a description of numerically the same individual, hence Spinoza's observation that "The mind and body, are one and the same individual, which at one time is considered under the attribute of thought, and at another under that of extension" (*E* II, 21S).

2.8

The human mind in itself is not distinct from the idea or ideas which are said to be in it. When I claim to know that some physical object exists in the external world, my knowledge is not directly knowledge of the physical object. Spinoza would say that it could not (logically) be. For a man to know the external world is for him to have ideas. To have ideas that constitute knowledge of the external world is for one's body to be affected by the external body. These affections themselves are modes of Extension; but there cannot be an affection in any body without there being a thought-object correlative with it, which alone is the object of a mind or consciousness. The body, whether my own, or other than my own, is not itself an object of thought or something thinkable. What is thinkable or capable of being the object of a mind is a mode of Thought in the sense of a thought-object.

I cannot become conscious of a body as *my* body except by being conscious of the effects which other bodies have on the one which I call my own. A child begins to be aware of its own body only upon coming into contact with physical objects other than itself. Its awareness of its own body is the awareness of the effects which other bodies have on its body. Thus to know other bodies is to know their effects on one's own body. These affections which one knows are not themselves bodies but thought-objects. Hence Spinoza's statement, "The human mind does not know the human body itself, nor does it know that the body exists, except through the ideas of the affections by which the body is affected" (*E* II, 19).

Since a man's mind consists of the ideas of the affections of his body as affected by other bodies, and his awareness of his body also consists of ideas correlated with the affections of his body, it follows that to refer to a man's mind or body is to refer to one and the same person, with the proviso that the nature of man as constituted of mind can be understood and explained only by reference to other factors or conditions belonging to the category to which he belongs as an individial having a mind. The nature of man as constituted of a body can be explained and understood only by reference to factors and conditions of the category to which he belongs as an individual having a body. One cannot meaningfully say that he has a body because he has a mind, any more than that he has a mind becuase he has a body. There is no causal relation between the two. Therefore, as Spinoza says, "The body cannot determine the mind to thought, neither can the mind determine the body to motion nor rest" (*E* III, 2). The 'cannot' in the proposition refers to a logical impossibility.

I do not wish to elaborate on the various theories of mind-body relation or to contrast Spinoza's view with them. I do, however, hope to have made clear in the above discussion that Spinoza's view about the nature of mind and the relation between mind and body defies a complete fit with any of the currently known theories of the subject.[4]

---

[4]For those interested in the topic, Douglas Odegard examines some of the differences and similarities between Spinoza's views and other current theories of the mind-body relation in his article on 'The Body Identical with the Human Mind: A Problem in Spinoza's Philosophy', in *Spinoza, Essays in Interpretation,* Maurice in Mandelbaum and Eugene Freeman, eds. (Illinois, Open Court, 1975), pp. 61–83. He also holds, as I do, that "Spinoza's general position on mind and body resists being placed in any of the categories commonly employed in philosophy of mind today" (Ibid., p. 68). There is perhaps one exception to this which has been suggested by Hilary Putnam (see his *Reason, Truth and History,* [Cambridge: Cambridge University Press 1981] pp. 84–85). He calls it 'synthetic identity of properties' and persusasively observes that such a view is "very much in line with Spinoza's thinking." In general I find Timothy Sprigge's views on mind-body relation in Spinoza's thought very illuminating (see *Inquiry,* Vol. 20, No. 4 [Winter 1977] pp. 419–445).

2.9

For Spinoza all ideas, as related to the human mind, are ideas of affections of the body; but the sense of 'idea' and the sense of 'affections of the body' needs a good deal of clarification in order to avoid a number of confusions. Ideas, which stand for all the different ways in which we acquire knowledge through sense perception, are not the same as ideas of reflection where there is no external body affecting one's own body. The kind of reflection one may be engaged in, for example, in trying to sort out what Spinoza might have understood as the notion of 'possibility' would be an instance of having this kind of idea, which is different from having a visual perception, say, of the book in front of me.

In the case of sense perception, when I am aware of the existence of an external object, this awareness or consciousness not only involves my having a body, but also involves another body which affects my body. Each and every body does not, of course, affect every other body in exactly the same way. The way one body affects another, and is in turn affected by it, depends upon individual constitutions and dispositions. For instance, the kind of awareness or idea I have of an external object necessarily involves the constitution and disposition not only of my own body, but also that of the body by which my body is being affected. My perception of the external world, therefore, is not just a one-way relation between an active agent, myself, and the passive object, the world outside me. In the experience of the world outside there is necessarily a two-way causal relation—between my body as it affects the external body and the external body as it affects my own. So that my idea or knowledge of the nature of external bodies and what they are like necessarily involves ideas or knowledge of the nature of my body or what my body is like.

However, we do sometimes experience illusions, hallucinations, and dreams, in which objects are experienced as though they were in the external world when they are not. In these experiences our bodies seem to be affected as though there were corresponding external bodies affecting our own. This shows that our knowledge of the kinds of things we experience as being outside ourselves, and which we seem to perceive through our senses, is indicative of the disposition and constitution of our own bodies rather than the nature of the bodies that we take to be outside. In either case, what we take to be outside ourselves depends upon the nature of our own bodies as they are affected by actual bodies, or by objects as bodies that seem to have actuality (see *E* II, 16, Dem., C1 and C2).

In the case of ideas of reflection, the kinds of affections or modifications of the body that are involved are the correlative and simultaneous changes occurring, in particular, in the nervous system, without which the process of ideation or thinking could not occur. The act of thinking is a mode of Thought correlated to the changes occurring in the body that are modes of Extension. Thus the order and connection of modes of thought corresponds to, is the same as, or is identical with the order and connection of modes of Extension.

2.10

So far, we have considerd only two senses of what Spinoza is to be understood to mean when he suggests that every idea or mode of Thought is an idea of an affection of the body. He also appears to hold that every mode of Extension has a correlated idea or mode of Thought, where the mode of Extension does not refer to changes occurring in the body of a person, nor does the term 'idea' refer to any act of thinking related to an individual having a mind. The question then arises in what sense of the term 'idea' can there be an idea correlated to the changes and modifications taking place in the physical universe which are not the object of thought in any individual mind?

No one would deny that innumerable physical changes are taking place in the universe, taken as a physical 'body', at any given moment. But Spinoza's view suggests that correlative to every such change as a mode of Extension there is necessarily an idea or a mode of Thought—even when no individual mind is thinking about it. Although these ideas are said to be 'in God', or 'in the infinite intellect of God', but since God is not a person, He cannot be said to have ideas in the sense of engaging in the activity of thinking or perceiving which applies only to human beings or other sentient creatures.

In order to understand Spinoza correctly here, it is necessary to examine his statement in *E* II, 32, where he says, "All ideas in so far as they are related to God, are true." He explains in the demonstration to the same proposition that, "All the ideas which are in God always agree with those things of which they are ideas, and therefore they are all ture." Spinoza appears to have in mind the following. The physical universe is constituted of certain kinds of facts, and to every such fact there corresponds a proposition, which Spinoza calls an 'idea'. This proposition or idea remains correlated with the fact even if no one is thinking about it. Nevertheless, insofar as it remains thinkable (i.e., something that can be thought), it is certainly a thought-object, and in that sense, an 'idea'. It follows that if a person's belief consists of an affirmation of a proposition or idea which correlates to the facts, then his belief is true. If one's belief constitutes an affirmation of some proposition other than the one that correlates to the facts, then one's belief is false. The truth of one's belief does not follow from the fact of one's affirmation or assertion of something to be the case. Truth or falsity of one's belief depends upon whether or not the content of one's belief is that proposition which correlates to the facts. There is thus a distinction between truth of one's belief (or the idea entertained by a mind), and the truth of a proposition (or idea as a thought-object). Clearly, the truth of a proposition or a thought-object, which is an idea that necesarily agrees with the thing of which it is an idea, does not depend upon whether one believes it to be true. For propositions (i.e., thought-objects or ideas taken in this sense), being ideas related to God, would "always agree with those things of which they are the ideas." Hence for every modification of Extension, or physical fact, there is a correlative ideas as a thinkble object, which is also capable of being thought by an individual mind. Since the term 'idea' is used by Spinoza to refer to both (1) the activity of thinking, as well as (2) the object of such activity which is a thought-object, it is only by taking it in the latter sense that one can understand his notion that all modes of Extension have correlative modes of Thought, and that the order and connection of ideas is the same as the order and connection of things.

2.11

We have observed that Spinoza uses the word 'idea' to refer to the thought-object as distinct from the 'idea' as being in the human mind. Furthermore, there are two kinds of thought-objects: (1) those correlated with the modifications of my body as affected by external bodies (the ideas of these thought-objects constitute my perceptual consciousness of the external world); and (2) those correlated with the nature of external bodies as they are, without affecting my body, in the sense just discussed. Spinoza seems to contend that it is only when ideas in an individual mind are ideas of thought-objects correlated with the nature of external bodies as they are, that an individual can be said to have true ideas.

The expression 'true idea', consequently, also refers to two different things. It can refer (1) to the *thought-object* correlated with the nature of an external body independently of being an idea in any finite mind; and (2) to the *idea in a finite mind,* which is the idea of the thought-object correlated with the nature of the external body. When Spinoza says in his essay *On the Improvement of the Understanding* "A true idea is something different from its correlate; thus a circle is different from the idea of a circle," the word 'idea', it should be clear, refers to the thought-object rather than to the idea in the human mind. He explains that "the idea of a circle is not something having a circumference and a centre, as a circle has; nor is the idea of a body that body itself" (*DIE*, 33). Because the thought-object is something different from its correlative body, it is capable of being understood through itself. Spinoza explains himself further with an example: The man Peter is something real. The true idea of Peter is the reality of Peter represented as an objective mode of thought and is itself something real and quite distinct from the spatio-temporal Peter:

> Now as this true idea of Peter is in itself something real, and has its own individual existence, it will also be capable of being understood—that is, of being the subject of another idea [idea in a human mind] which will contain by representation all that the idea [the thought-object] of Peter contains actually. (*DIE,* 33)

From this it would seem to follow that since my perception of my body (as existing) consists of ideas of the thought-objects correlated with my body as a spatio-temporal entity, it is in principle impossible that my idea or knowledge of its existence not be a true idea. Consequently, as Spinoza says, "The human body exists as we perceive it" (*E* II, 13, C). Furthermore, if my perception of objects in the external world consists of ideas in my mind of thought-objects correlated with the affections of my body which are causally connected with the external body, then it is impossible for any idea in my mind which constitutes veridical perception to be an instance of false knowledge.

2.12

An account of Spinoza's view of 'error' would further clarify his conception of 'true idea'. There is a distinction between the idea that a man, say, Peter, has of his own existence (consisting of ideas of thought-objects correlated with the affections of his own body), and the idea of Peter's existence that another man, say, Paul, has (which are ideas of the thought-objects correlated with the affections of Paul's body). It is possible for Paul to have ideas of thought-objects correlated with the nature of his own body, and to believe that Peter exists, even if Peter in fact does not exist. In other words, Paul can have ideas representing Peter as an externally existing entity, even when Peter does not exist. But it is in priniciple impossible for Peter to have ideas of the affections of his own body, unless there is a body whose affections are correlated with thought-objects whose ideas constitute Peter's mind. For, as Spinoza puts it elsewhere, "idea of the mind is united to the mind in the same way as the mind itself is united to the body" (*E* II, 21).[5] So, although Paul can perceive Peter when Peter ex-

[5]That is to say, for a person to understand the nature of the mind (i.e., to have the idea of the mind) is for him to acknowledge that the mind is the idea of the body. Since for aperson to understand anything is for him to entertain an idea of the thought-object correalted with thenature of the thing of which

ists, and can also imagine that Peter exists when he does not, it is impossible for Peter to perceive or imagine his own body when it does not exist.

So long as Paul merely imagines Peter to exist (when he does not, or no longer does), Paul is not making an error. But he will be in error if on the basis of this idea he believes that Peter not only exists as an idea of his imagination, but also exists as a spatio-temporal entity. For then Paul's mind, in not having an idea of the thought-object correlated with the nonexistence of Peter's body, entertains a false idea of Peter's existence. This is what Spinoza means, I believe, when he refers to Paul in the above example and observes, "These imaginations of the mind regarded by themselves contain no error, and . . . the mind is not in error because it imagines, but only insofar as it is considered as wanting in an idea which excludes the existence of those things which it imagines as present' (*E* II, 17S). "There is something real in the ideas themselves," Spinoza says, "whereby the true are distinguished from the false" (*DIE*, 70). This reality must belong, clearly, to ideas as thought-objects rather than to ideas as constituting the human mind. As Spinoza points out, "If an architect conceives a building properly constructed, even if such a building may never have existed, and may never exist, nevertheless the idea is true; and the idea remains the same whether it be put into execution or not" (*DIE* 69). If one considers the above two statements together then not only is the architect's idea true

---

it is the thought-object, it is in principle impossible for a person to have a true idea of the nature of mind without acknowledging that one cannot be conscious without one's consciousness being necessarily correlated with the modifications and changes occurring in his body. Hence to understand the nature of the mind is to know that the mind is necessarily related to the (modifications of the) body. This is the same as to say the 'idea of the mind is united to the mind in the same way as the mind itself is united to the body.'

whether the building is built or not, but the idea is also true whether he continues to think it or not. What makes the architect's idea true is the nature of the idea as a thought-object, and not the fact that it exists as a thought in his mind.

A man's perception, then, of external bodies can occur only *through* ideas correlated with the affections of his body. To perceive an external body as actually existing is not the same as imagining it to exist, in the sense in which Paul imagined Peter's body to exist when in fact it did not. It is only insofar as the mind imagines external bodies in the above sense, that it does not possess a true idea of them (*E* II, 26 Dem.). It is important to remember that Spinoza is not rejecting all knowledge derived from sense perception as false.[6] The demonstration of *E* II, 26 says, "When the human mind through the ideas of the affections of its body contemplates external bodies, we say that it then imagines." Spinoza refers here to *E* II, 17S, where, in explainig his use of the term 'imagine', he says, "We will give to those affections of the human body, the ideas of which represent to us external bodies as if they were present, the name of *images of things*, although they do not actually reproduce the forms of things. When the mind contemplates bodies in this way, we will say that it imagines." And if this is what imagining means, then he is, of course, correct in saying that, "So far as the mind imagines external bodies it does not possess an adequate knowledge of them" (*E* II, 26 Dem.).

2.13

There is one other point Spinoza discusses in the *Treatise on the Improvement of the Understanding* that is significant here. We would

---

[6]Cf. C.De.Deugd, *The Significance of Spinoza's First Kind of Knowledge*

all agree that if, on the basis of the ideas of his imagination, Paul believes Peter to exist (when in fact Peter does not), then he is entertaining a false belief. Spinoza, however, goes further. He suggests that if Paul made a statement asserting the existence of Peter, without knowing whether Peter in fact did or did not exist, then Paul's statement, as far as Paul is concerned, is false, even if Peter did exist. "The assertion that Peter exists is true only with regard to him who knows for certain that Peter does exist" (*DIE*, 69). The question is whether Spinoza means that Paul's statement is false because Paul does not have the evidence required for his statement to be true. If this is what he means, then he may be implying a distinction between merely asserting or making a statement, and believing or entertaining something or having an idea. Perhaps Spinoza has in mind that just as one may entertain an idea or believe a proposition without stating it, one may also state or assert a proposition without believing it. I might, for instance, entertain various thoughts, beliefs (i.e., ideas) about, say, immortality or life after death without stating (uttering or writing) them. I might also utter the sentence and thereby state that 'the chair I am sitting on is on fire,' without believing that the chair is, in fact, on fire. Or I might simply make a verbal mistake in the course of making a statement of my belief. The grounds for the falsity of belief, then, may not be the grounds for the falsity of the statement. Another example he gives would tend to support this reading. "When I heard a man lately complaining that his court had flown into one of his neighbor's fowls," says Spinoza, "I understood what he meant and therefore did not imagine him to be in error" (*E* II, 47S).

(Netherlands, 1966), where his whole thesis appears to be to establish this point, with which I happen to agree.

Here, he suggests that although the man's statement was false, there was no error in his belief.

There is little doubt that he does have this distinction in mind, but it is unlikely that this is all he means. I think that he further means that the grounds which make a belief true (or true ideas) are also the grounds which make the statement of those beliefs true statements. If Spinoza were asked, "What does it mean for someone to know for certain that an idea is true?" he would have to say that the idea of Peter, in *my* mind, is true if it is the idea of the thought-object correlated with the actual existence or nonexistence of Peter. The man who asserts that Peter exists without knowing it for certain, makes a statement which is not evidentially but only accidentally related to (the thought-object of) Peter's actual existence. So that, although what is asserted or stated (namely a proposition) taken in itself is true, the man who asserted it did not have in mind the idea of the appropriate correlative thought-object. It is the lack of an evidentially appropriate relation between the idea in the man's mind and the thought-object correlated with Peter's existence which explains the falsity of his statement. It is also the lack of such a relation between what Paul imagines and believes to be the case (when he imagines Peter to exist when he does not), and the thought-object correlated with Peter's nonexistence, that makes Paul's belief a false belief.

2.14

Further light is shed on this point by considering Spinoza's discussion of the notions of 'truth' and 'falsity' in the *Short Treatise.* In speaking of these notions he says, "Truth is an affirmation (or denial) made about a certain thing which agrees with that same thing; and falsity is an affirmation (or denial) about a thing which does not agree with that thing" (*ST* II, 15). This statement raises questions which require further consideration.

First, what exactly counts as an affirmation or a denial? Spinoza's view seems to be that to affirm something or to deny something, (e.g., the sun is larger in mass than the moon, or the sun is not larger in mass than the moon), is not simply a matter of uttering or writing the words in the form of a sentence. Spinoza seems to think that affirmation and denial cen be carried out without utterance or external expression of any kind. Affirmation or denial, he suggests, involve entertaining ideas, thoughts, or beliefs. To affirm that the sun is larger than the moon is to think, or believe, or have an idea that the sun is larger than the moon, which, of course, can also be expressed in language. It is not, however, the expression of the sentence uttered, written, or gestured that is true or false. Rather, it is the idea, or thought, or belief, that finds expression though the uttered or written sentence that is true or false. I can thus affirm or deny an idea without uttering or writing anything or expressing it in any other form. For this reason, in speaking of truth and falsity, Spinoza invariably mentions true or false *ideas* (see *DIE*, 33ff.), or, as in *E* I, Ax. 6, "A true idea must agree with that of which it is an idea." That is to say, affirming something about a thing which does not agree with the thing itself is the same as entertaining a false idea or belief or thought about that thing. This also suggests that as truth and falsity apply to affirmations and denials, and to affirm or deny something is to entertain ideas, therefore, ideas alone can be said to be either true or false and not the things of which they are ideas.

What sort of entities then, if they are entities, are the things with which an affirmation or an idea is supposed to agree (leaving aside for the moment the notion of 'agreement' to which we shall turn later)? What sort of examples can we find to clarify the notion of 'things' here? Spinoza does say that "All things which are in Nature, are either things or actions" (*ST* I, 10). This would mean that he places things and actions into two different logical types. Since we are concerned here with things and not actions, it is possible to understand him as saying that things are simply objects given to us through sense experience. Therefore, whatever is not an object of actual or possible sense experience is not a thing. This must not be, however, what he understands by the term 'thing'; for he also speaks, for instance, of things of reason *(entia rationis),* eternal things, and fictitious things, things that are possible, impossible, or necessary. We can speak of miracles or ghosts, and either affirm or deny their existence. So there can be things that we can talk about, but which may not exist. Then there are things that we talk about which are also things that exist. There may also be things that exist that we have no ideas about and hence do not have any way of talking about them. Spinoza would say that in talking about God and attributes, we are talking about some 'thing'. He also speaks of a true idea as being different from its correlate *(ideatum).* Thus a circle is different from the idea of a circle, in that an idea of a circle is not something having a circumference and a center as a circle has. Nor is the idea of a body that body itself (*DIE* 33). Both, nevertheless, can be said to be 'things', though, indeed, not of the same kind.

It seems that the things with which ideas are supposed to agree in order for them to be true, are taken by Spinoza in a very general way to be any objects of reference, and not necessarily extra-linguistic reference. So that if I know, for instance, what someone is referring to when he speaks of things that are impossible by correctly answering, "he is referring to things like round squares," then round squares fall into the category of 'things'. Round squares do not have to exist in order for them to be 'things' in the sense of 'objects of reference'. Hampshire rightly observes that "To know what you are referring to, or speaking about, is not the same as to know that there exists something to which you are referring; you may not intend to refer to something which actually exists; you may intend to refer to something fictitious, imaginary or logically impossible. The linguistic act of referring is the same in each case and is so far non-committal in respect of existence."[7]

Now, if by 'things' is meant 'any object of reference', whether imaginary, fictitious, perceptual, real, impossible, necessary, or whatever, then any affirmation or denial will have to agree in some sense with something that the affirmation or denial is about. The affirmation or denial or idea involved in saying "There are no round squares" is true; and the affirmation 'round squares exist' is false; but what kind of thing or fact can Spinoza have in mind with which its agreement or lack of agreement makes one true and the other false?

It will be admitted that when we claim "there are no round squares", we are denying that there is an extra-linguistic reference of the linguistic 'thing', namely, the term 'round squares'. In addition, to claim, "round squares exist" is to affirm that the term 'round squares' has an extra-linguistic reference. There is nothing in Spinoza's writings that would be inconsistent with his answer if he were to say that the agreement or lack of agreement here with the fact or thing that makes one idea or affirmation true and the other false is that it is in the nature of self-

---

[7]Cf. S. Hampshire, "Identification and Existence," in *Contemporary British Philosophy,* Third Series, Ed. H.D. Lewis. London; Allen & Unwin, 1956, p. 203.

contradictory linguistic terms, such as 'round squares', to lack existential reference.

2.15

Another important point which is not generally understood is that there is a difference in Spinoza's thought between inadequacy or uncertainty of an idea and its falsity, as well as between its adequacy and its truth. In *E* II, 29C Spinoza points out that the human mind, when it perceives things in the common order of nature, has no adequate knowledge of external bodies, but only a confused and mutilated (or inadequate) knowledge. Furthermore, he contends that the human mind perceives external bodies as existing only through the ideas of the affections of its body (*E* II, 26). This, however, does not amount to saying that whenever we perceive external bodies as actually existing we are involved in making an error. Error, or false knowledge, consists in the absence of that certainty which is the defining characteristic of an adequate idea, and this certainty is more than a mere psychological certainty. It is quite common for a person to feel psychologically certain and yet entertain a false idea. The criterion for the adequacy of an idea is that it be one which, considered in itself without reference to the object, has all the properties or internal signs of a true idea (*E* II, Df. 4). The notion of adequate idea in Spinoza's thought seems to exclude all reference to the agreement of the idea with an object, as is clear from the explanation added to *E* II, Df. 4, which says "I say internal, so as to exclude that which is external, the agreement, namely of the idea with its ideatum." Also, the certainty that is involved in having an adequate idea is not based upon the negative criterion of absence of doubt, or grounds for doubt (*E* II, 49S) but on the positive criterion of 'seeing' its truth to be undeniable on any grounds (*E*

II, 43 and S). It is on these grounds of internal self-consistency that an adequate idea must be a true idea.

It is this kind of adequate idea or knowledge, which is necessarily true, that belongs to what Spinoza describes as reason or intuition. He also says (as noted earlier) that the human body exists as we perceive it (*E* II, 13C), in spite of the fact that our perception of it from the common order of nature is inadequate. However, Spinoza could not, and does not mean that his knowledge of the existence of the human body, as it is derived from sense perception, is false. It may, of course, be a case of inadequate knowledge. While he does say that falsity or error occurs only at the level of the first kind of knowledge, namely 'opinion or imagination' (*E* II, 41)—which must include sense perception—it does not follow that all knowledge at this level is necessarily false. Imagination and perception by themselves, he tells us, contain no error or falsity (*E* II, 17S). Rather, falsity or error arises when one assents to, asserts, or believes in the existence of what one merely imagines or perceives to be the case, without having excluded all those ideas which might lead one to believe something on inadequate and inappropriate evidence. Spinoza's thought may perhaps be expressed as follows. From the fact that one has an adequate idea, it follows that one must also have a feeling of certainty about its truth. From the fact, however, that one feels certain, it does not follow that the idea which is entertained is an adequate idea. In every case of a person's entertaining a true idea, he must also feel certain about its truth. Yet this certainty may be a consequence of having the evidence required for the idea to be true, and this evidence may involve reference to something other than or external to the idea itself. But a true idea is an adequate idea only if its certainty does not require reference to any object other than the idea itself. This was the distinction, it seems, that Spinoza wished to draw when he wrote to Tschirnhaus (*Ep* 60), "I recognize no other difference between a true and an adequate idea than that the word true refers to the agreement of the idea with its ideatum, while the word adequate refers to the nature of the idea itself." If this is the distinction he is making, then Spinoza would appear to hold that an idea may be true even though it may not be adequate. This would explain the assertion that the human body does exist as we perceive it. Nothing in Spinoza's discussion of inadequate knowledge gives the reader grounds for believing that Spinoza was dismissing the external world, or our veridical perception of it, as a mere illusion.

2.16

To perceive things truly, that is to say, to have ideas which are ideas of thought-objects correlated with the nature and constitution of things as they are in themselves, is to have rational knowledge. Rational knowledge, or 'knowledge in accordance with reason,' consists precisely in seeing, grasping, or understanding the necessary relation between ideas in one's own mind and thought-objects correlated with the nature of things as they are. This is what Spinoza means when he says, "It is of the nature of reason to consider things as necessary and not as contingent. This necessity of things it perceives truly; that is to say, as it is in itself" (*E* II, 44 Dem.). And to perceive things truly, he points out, is to have an idea which agrees with that of which it is an idea (*E* I, A6). The necessity of this relation between a true idea in a mind and a thought-object is the same as the necessity of the divine nature of God, referred to earlier. It is, he is suggesting, the nature of the universe, and the nature of the principle of its origin, that to know things truly is to know the necessary relation between ideas in one's mind and the thought-objects correlative to the things constituting the world.

The foundation of rational knowledge is that a human being knows with certainty that he has a body and that he has ideas, or is conscious. As all ideas in the human mind are ideas of affections of the body, it is in principle impossible for a man to be conscious of these ideas (or have ideas of ideas) without the correlative changes occurring in his body. Hence, in being conscious of having ideas, or in being self-conscious, he is necessarily affirming not merely the existence of ideas, but also the existence of his body. His body is only one mode of extension among infinite others, all of which are, equally, extended objects. The fact that we know objects as extended, logically implies that extension is an attribute forming a necessary part of the nature of our knowledge of the universe. It is not merely a category under which we perceive bodies; it must also form an essential part of the nature of the principle of origin of the universe, by reference to which alone it can be explained why certain things are bodies, rather than anything else.

The knowledge a human mind has of bodies—not this or that particular body, but as modes of extension, and of ideas as modes of thought—is knowledge that cannot be false, and hence is adequate knowledge. It belongs to the category of 'common notions' in the sense that I, in having a body, also know those common properties (of extension) which form the essential character of other bodies. It is by having this common nature that my body is both capable of being, and in fact is, affected by other bodies, the ideas of whose thought-objects constitute my mind. What makes 'common notions' true, however, is not just the fact that their ideas are present in a human mind. Common notions refer to "things which are common to everything" (*E* II, 38), as well as to their correlated thought-objects. Thinking or affirming or having ideas of these thought-objects constitutes adequate ideas in an individual mind.

Because the nature of *natura naturans,* the 'source' or 'origin', the primal reality, is such that the universe as its manifestation, *natura naturata,* is constituted the way it is, therefore, the intellect perceives the nature of that reality by experiencing the world under two distinct categories of thought and extension. My knowledge of the world, as consisting of physical objects and thought-objects, constitutes ideas which cannot be anything but adequate and true; for these ideas are logically related to the thought-objects of which they are ideas. Because it is impossible for an effect to follow if there is no determinate condition or explanation for it (*E* I, A3), the ideas we have in our minds are effects whose nature can be understood only in terms of conditions that explain them. When we know these conditions as they are, and the necessity of their relation to the ideas in our mind, it is logically impossible for our knowledge of these universal conditions to be inadequate or false. Once we have an initial idea that is adequate and true, then other ideas logically related to them will have to be ideas of thought-objects reflecting the causal relations between correlated modes of Extension. These common notions, and other ideas logically related to them, are thought-objects of things as they are in themselves. They do not pertain to the nature of any one given individual, but to the nature of all things considered under a given category. In this sense, common notions—being thought-objects correlated with the actual nature of the universe, and to actual properties of things in the universe without reference to any time or place—are universally true notions.

A corollary to this would be that two individual minds entertaining such universal ideas cannot but agree with each other.

The question of difference of opinion among them about the truth of these ideas cannot (logically) arise.

2.17

If asked "How can one be certain that the ideas one has are not merely true but also adequate?" Spinoza would answer: If one is asking for a criterion to determine the adequacy of ideas, which is separate from the ideas in question, then there can be no other criteria except such ideas themselves. They are adequate and true for the simple reason that, being ideas of thought-objects correlated with the actual nature of things, they could not (logically) be false or inadequate. They are their own criteria of truth. Their logical certainty is also the ground for their psychological certainty, hence, "He who has a true idea knows at the same time that he has a true idea, nor can he doubt the truth of the thing" (*E* II, 43). (By 'true idea' here, Spinoza must mean an idea which is at once adequate *and* true.) This answer tends to generate a certain degree of confusion. One is not quite certain whether Spinoza has really answered the question, or what the question is that he takes himself to be dealing with. It calls for further consideration.

There is no doubt that by saying that " . . . [f]or the cer titude of truth, no further sign is necessary beyond the possession of a true idea" (*DIE*, 35), Spinoza is responding to the question of whether a person can be certain, and if so, how it is possible to be certain that an idea he takes to be true is a true idea and not a false one. The question as to how one can be sure that one is not making a mistake is a legitimate one, and Spinoza recognizes its significance. It is also important to keep in mind that this question is quite different from another question with which Spinoza is not directly concerned; namely, whether I can be certain, and how it is possible for me to be certain, that the idea that *you* claim to entertain, or *he* claims to entertain, is a true idea. It seems that for Spinoza this second question is answerable in some sense that is not entirely clear, only in terms of the first, and not independently of it.

His answer to the first question is that this is a special kind of question to which his answer is the only correct one: "In order to know that I know I must first know" (*DIE*, 34). This statement my be unnecessarily cryptic and seems to involve an am biguity in the use of the term 'know'. What he means is that in order to be certain an idea is true, I must first have a true idea. That is to say, in order for me to raise the question about whether I know what I think is true, it is necessary for me to have a conception of what counts as a true idea by actually having a true idea. It would not do to seek a prior criterion that could then be applied to determine the truth of an idea; for such a criterion, if it were available, will itself presuppose knowing what a true idea is. However, once we do have a true idea we do not need any *other* criterion to determine its truth. For a true idea understood in this way is, indeed, its own criterion, and, therefore, as Spinoza puts it, "Truth at once reveals itself and also what is false" (*ST* II, 15).[8]

Spinoza not only says that "In order to know that I know, I must first know", but he also distinguishes this from the statement "In order to know, there is no need to know that we know" (*DIE*, 34). In order to appreciate the full significance of the first statement it is necessary to understand what he means by the lat-

---

[8]Spinoza makes the same point in *E* II, 43 S by saying " . . . what can be clearer or more certain than a true idea as the standard of truth? Just as light reveals both itself and the darkness, so truth is the standard of itself and of the false."

ter. And the examples that he gives to explain it seem to suggest that he means the following.

In order for me to be certain that an object of my reflection is, say, Peter—an actually existing individual—I do not need to refer to a criterion of certainty to determine whether what I am certain of (namely, that I am thinking of Peter) is really that of which I am certain. In order for me to be certain, in other words, that the idea I am entertaining is that of Peter, as distinct from anyone else, I do not need to ascertain further whether it is Peter that I am thinking of. *I* do not need to ask *myself*, under these circumstances, the question "What makes me sure that I am really thinking of Peter?" in the sense that someone *else* might ask me, under the same circumstances, "What makes you so sure that you are thinking of Peter and not of Paul?" For, in order for me to know or to be certain that I am thinking of Peter, all I need to do is to think of Peter. That is to say, in order to know (that I am thinking of Peter) there is no need to know *that I know this.* No further sign is necessary for me to be certain of this "beyond the possession of the true idea." Hence, "In order to know that I know, I must first know."

Certainty is held by Spinoza to be identical with entertaining or thinking, or possessing thoughts which are correlated with the things that constitute the universe. Spinoza, in fact, identifies certainty with possession of adequate ideas or *essentia objectiva* of a thing (*DIE*, 35). An adequate idea is, in other words, the thought-object (or objective essence) of a thing, whch is capable of being made an object of reflection without reference to its actual correlate or that of which it is the thought. It is "an idea which insofar as it is considered in itself, without reference to the object [i.e., its correlate] has all the properties or internal signs [*denominationes intrinsicas*] of a true idea" (*E* II, D4). To this he adds, "I say internal, so as to exclude that which is external, the agreement, namely, of the idea with its object" (*E* II, D4, Expl.). This addition is intended obviously, to clarify the relation, as well as the distinction, between true ideas and adequate ideas. The suggestion is that the terms 'adequate' and 'inadequate', with respect to ideas, are used to draw attention to the nature of the idea itself (i.e., to the objective essence, the thought-object); whereas the terms 'true' and 'false' are used to refer to the *relation* of an idea entertained by an individual (mind) and the objective essence or thought-object. Thus, my thinking or believing something, or having an idea, is true if it agrees with that of which it is an idea (*E* I, Ax.6). Whereas, in the case of adequate ideas as those that are necessarily correlated with the nature of things as they are, the question whether they do or do not agree with that of which they are ideas simply does not arise.

2.18

For Spinoza the goal of understanding is to discern and distinguish a true idea from all other perceptions. The method of understanding, therefore, consists in reflective knowledge, or reflection on objects as thought-objects or "the idea of an idea." Since one cannot think of thought-objects unless there are thought-objects, it follows that there can be no understanding without granting thought-objects (*DIE*, 38). There is a remarkably close similarity here between Spinoza's views and those of Frege's. What Frege calls 'thoughts', and what I call 'thought-objects', are what Spinoza calls 'adequate ideas', '*essentia objectiva*', or sometimes simply 'ideas'.[9]

For Frege, understanding consists of 'grasping of thoughts',

---

[9]At times he also calls them 'thoughts', as, for example, in *DIE* 73.

an activity which requires "a special mental capacity, the power of thinking".[10] This special mental capacity is what Spinoza refers to as 'reasoning', 'reason', or 'understanding'. Frege appears to have divined Spinoza's mind remarkably well in the following passage.

> In thinking we do not produce thoughts, we grasp them. For what I have called Thoughts stand in the closest connection with truth. What I acknowledge as true, I judge to be true quite apart from my acknowledging its truth or even thinking about it. That someone thinks it has nothing to do with the truth of a Thought. "Facts, facts, facts" cries the scientist if he wants to bring home the necessity of a firm foundation for science. What is a fact? A fact is a thought that is true. But the scientist will surely not acknowledge something to be the firm foundation of science if it depends on men's varying states of consciousness. The work of science does not consist in creation, but in the discovery of true thoughts. The astronomer can apply a mathematical truth in the investigation of long past events which took place when—on Earth at least—no one had yet recognized that truth. He can do this because the truth of a thought is timeless. Therefore that truth can not have come to be only upon discovery.[11]

If we agree with Frege, that to think or to understand is to grasp a thought, then the moment at which we think a thought does have time specification, but what we think at that moment, namely the thought, is timeless. It is not something that has temporal dimension. The expression of thought in a sentence must also have time specification in order for it to succeed in expressing or communicating a thought (or for it to 'contain' a thought); but the thought thus expressed, if it is true, is true

---

[10]Frege, *Logical Investigations,* p. 25.

[11]Ibid.

timelessly. The phrase 'is true', properly understood when used in any context, does not refer to the speaker's present. As Frege suggests, the present tense in 'is true' which is involved in the expression of the grasping of a thought and its assertion, is a tense of timelessness. Spinoza would express the same idea in his rather cryptic but profound way by saying "It is of the nature of reason to perceive things under a certain form of eternity" (*E* II 44, C2). To put this another way, if that which is timelessly true is not subject to changing conditions, then there is a sense in which it is true not contingently but necessarily. One can understand, therefore, why Spinoza should say "It is not of the nature of reason to consider things as contingent but as necessary" (*E* II, 44).

2.19

Our confidence in our ability or power to understand, to form true ideas, or to 'grasp thoughts' increases in proportion to our entertaining ideas or thinking thoughts correlative to things that actually exist in nature. It follows that a complete understanding would include comprehending ideas correlated with the whole order of nature. This is what Spinoza appears to suggest when he says "The more things the mind knows, the better does it understand its own strength and the order of nature," and a mind will be "absolutely perfect when it gains a knowledge of the absolutely perfect being" (*DIE* 40).

Now, since thought-objects have an objective reality of their own, and all thought-objects—as ideas that are necessarily true—correspond to their correlates in the order of nature, then the order and connection of ideas as thought-objects in the realm of thoughts (as modes of thought), will likewise have their corresponding correlates in the order of nature. Or as Spinoza puts it, "The ratio existing between two ideas [i.e., thought-objects] is the same as the ratio between the actual realities corresponding to those ideas" (*DIE* 39). In other words "The order and connection of ideas is the same as the order and connection of things" (*E* II, 7).

Furthermore, Spinoza points out (and this is how his theory of knowledge may be seen to be related to his metaphysics) that "In order to reproduce in every respect the faithful image of nature, our mind must deduce all its ideas from the idea which represents the origin and source of the whole of nature, so that it may itself become the source of other ideas" (*DIE* 42). There is hardly any doubt that the referent of 'the origin and source of the whole of nature' is the same as that of 'God' or 'all the attributes'.

Why does Spinoza think it is necessary that, in order for the system of ideas which constitute the human mind to represent the order of nature faithfully, all our ideas must be deducible from the idea of the origin or source of the whole of nature? The only possible answer would seem to be that the 'source' or the 'origin' is the ultimate reality and the grounds without which an individual thing, in the common order of nature, could not possibly exist. The common order of nature is the consequence of the nature of the source or the origin. The relation between ground and consequence is analogous to, but not identical with, the relation between cause and effect. This difference is expressed by the statement that "God is the immanent cause of everything." That is to say, the reality of the 'source' and the existence of everything else follows from the essential nature of the 'source' in a way similar to the one in which an effect follows from a cause. Since knowledge of an effect depends upon and involves the knowledge of the cause, every increase in our understanding of the cause-effect sequence in the order of nature amounts to an increase in our knowledge of the source or origin, or the first cause, or God.[12]

[12]Cf. footnote to *DIE* 92. "It is . . . manifest that we can not understand anything of nature without at the same time increasing our knowledge of the first cause, or God."

Chapter Three

Action

3.1

Every particular thing, for Spinoza, is an affection or mode of one or the other attribute expressed in a determinate manner. Each particular thing depends, for the explanation of the kind of thing it is, upon the nature of the primal reality itself, and for its existence in the common order of nature upon some other particular things as its causal condition. Each individual thing, by its very nature, makes an effort to maintain its being or endeavors to preserve itself and its own nature. This effort, tendency, drive, or endeavor to persist in its being is that thing's *conatus,* which "is nothing but the actual essence of the thing itself" (*E* III, 7). This is what makes any particular thing the individual it is. A man's *conatus* consists of two kinds of effort. One is related to him as an individual having a mind, and is called 'will'. The other is related to him as an individual composed of both mind and body, and is called 'appetite' (*E* III, 9S).

The human mind comprises ideas which are clear and distinct, hence adequate and true, as well as ideas of imagination, perception, and sensation, most of which are inadequate and hence confused (*E* III, 9 Dem.). The effort of a human being, as a psycho-physical organism, is directed towards preserving his own interests and identity in relation to the external world. His desires, therefore, being conditioned or determined by this effort, are a conscious manifestation of his *conatus.* In this sense 'desire' may be said to be "appetite of which a man is conscious" (*E* III, 9S).

The *conatus* of man, when related to his mind alone, described by Spinoza as 'will', refers to the tendency of the human mind not simply to have ideas, but to have ideas, it would seem, which are adequate and true. For the will and intellect to be identical (*E* II, 49C), the 'will' must refer to the active character of the mind as distinct from the passive reception of ideas of imagination, perception, or sensation. Now to have adequate ideas, as noted earlier, is to have ideas that can be explained or understood without reference to anything other than themselves. The mind is active when it has adequate ideas; but to say that a mind is active is the same as saying that ideas in the mind are self-explanatory or self-evident, or that a human being, as an individual having such a mind, is self-determining or free. To have such a mind is the same as to have ideas which are logically related to thought-objects correlative with the nature of things as they are.

3.2

Spinoza's definition of 'action' needs a careful look at this stage. He says that "we act when anything is done either within us or without us, of which we are the adequate cause [an adequate cause being one whose effect can be clearly and distinctly understood by means of the cause (*E* III, Df. 1)], that is to say, when from our nature anything follows, either within us or without us, which by that nature alone can be clearly and distinctly understood" (*E* III, Df. 2).

The term 'we' in this definition, does not refer just to the body or to the mind alone, but to an individual human being or a person as a psycho-physical organism—or to man as composed of both mind and body. So 'action' is, properly, a term that has to be used with respect to a person as a whole, and not with respect to a person as merely having a mind or as merely having a body. It does not make sense to speak of the mind of a person having performed an action any more than it makes sense to speak of the body of a person having performed an action. Actions, in other words, are ascribable to individuals who can be said to have both mind and body. Since there are beings other than human beings who can also be said to be individuals having a mind and a body (and indeed there is a sense in which, insofar as every body Spinoza takes to be "animated, though in different degrees" [*E* II, 13S], every thing that has a body may also be said to have a mind, in a rather special sense of the term 'mind' or 'idea'), the *kind* of mind, in combination with a body, that is required, in order for an individual having such a mind and body to be ascribed an *action*, calls for specification. An individual psycho-physical organism, Spinoza tells us, can be said to have performed an action "when anything takes place either within us or outside us of which we are the adequate cause". Here again the term 'us' in 'within us' (*in nobis*) and 'outisde us' or 'external to us' (*extra nos*) clearly refers to persons or individuals having both mind and body.

There are two kinds of things that can be happening 'inside us' as psycho-physical organisms: some physical changes and modifications can be occurring inside our body, and we can also be having certain experiences or ideas that are correlated with certain changes and motions taking place within our body. Obviously, there are a number of movements of various sorts that are constantly occurring within our bodies which can also be thought of, but which are not, at any given moment, the object of our consciousness. The sense in which these movements *can* be objects of our consciousness but are not necessarily present to our mind, are thought-objects, and hence 'ideas' in *one* sense of the term. These physical movements in the body have causal relations with other physical movements in the body by reference to which they can be understood as effects. Insofar as the movements within our bodies are causally related to other physical movements within our own bodies alone—without involving any other physical objects outside our bodies—the internal physical changes that cause other physical changes can be said to be the 'adequate cause' of such changes. Since a number of such modifications in our bodies related in a cause-effect chain continue to occur without our being aware of them, we, as persons (i.e., as having not merely a body but also a mind), cannot be said to be their causes. That is to say, it is not because we have a mind therefore these physical changes are taking place in the body. These changes take place despite our having a mind, and hence these changes cannot be said to be our actions. They are not something that we can be said to be doing, but rather something that is happening. They are events, in other words, and not actions. For, as noted earlier, in order for an action to be ascribed to an individual, the individual must be regarded not merely as having a body, or merely as having a mind, but as having both body and mind.

There is, nevertheless, a sense of the term 'act' or 'active' which can be applied to a person while referring either to his body or to his mind. In this sense of 'act' a person's body can be said to be 'active' insofar as the movements connected with his body can be explained by reference to other movements connected with his own body ('explained' here is used in the sense covered by the notion of 'adequate cause', namely, a cause through which its effect can be clearly and distinctly understood).

Correspondingly, a person's mind can be said to be 'active' when an idea or a set of ideas constituting his mind can be clearly and distinctly understood by their relation to other ideas or sets of ideas constituting that mind. Since an idea in a mind is true, as we have seen, if it is the idea of the thought-object correlated to the nature of things as they are, and every thought-object, as an idea being correlated with the nature of things as they are, is necessarily an idea that is to be taken as *intrinsically* true (*E* II, Df. 4), a mind will be said to be 'active' insofar as the ideas constituting it are adequate ideas. Hence Spinoza's statement that insofar as our mind "has adequate ideas it is necessarily active, and insofar as it has inadequate ideas, it is necessarily passive" (*E* III, 1).

For a person to have performed an action, in the strict sense, whatever he is said to have 'done' must be related to the adequate ideas in his mind and to the conscious movements of his body that are correlated with them. It also follows that if what a person is said to have 'done' is related to ideas constituting his mind that are inadequate, then, to the extent that what he has done does not count as 'action' he is not active but passive. So if a mind has inadequate ideas, the corresponding activity of the body will be an 'inadequate action'.

Furthermore, the more the human mind is constituted of confused and inadequate ideas, the less they reflect the knowledge of thought-objects of the state of affairs in the world as they actually are. The less the knowledge in the human mind reflects the nature of things as they are, the more confused and inadequate the individual's responses will be with respect to the world. The order and connection of ideas in the human mind are correlated to the modifications of the body; and an increase in the active power of the mind has correlated affections or modifications of the body which, in turn, increase its active power. Insofar as the activities of a human being (considered as an individual having a body) are correlated to him as an individual having a mind composed of adequate ideas, he is self-determining and, in this sense, free.

One cannot (logically) refer to a person's mind or body without referring to him as an individual composed of mind *and* body. So, one cannot meaningfully say that a person's mind has adequate ideas without necessarily implying that the corresponding activity of his body can be clearly understood by reference to the nature of his own body. Now if the relation between adequate ideas in a human mind is a relation which is *logically* necessary, then the relation between correlative affections of the body must be one that is *causally* necessary. So an individual human being would be said to be 'free' when the adequate and true ideas in his mind that are logically related to each other have correlative activities of his body that are causally related to each other. These two descriptions refer to one and the same individual from two distinct points of view.

Since by 'reality' and 'perfection' Spinoza means one and the same thing (*E* II, D6), the more 'active' a person is, in both mind and body, and therefore more self-determining and free he is, the more 'real' or 'perfect' he is as an individual. Hence his statement, "The more perfection a thing possesses, the more it acts . . . and conversely the more it acts the more perfect it is" (*E* V, 40). As the reality and perfection of a thing depends on its activity and freedom, it is indeed true, as Hampshire observed in his British Academy lecture, that for Spinoza the fundamental term of evaluation is not the word 'good' but the word 'free'.[1] Spinoza explains human action not by reference to the notion of choice between alternative ends which a man is free to make, or to the concept of volition, but by reference to the mind's activity and passivity, or the adequacy and inadequacy of ideas which a man entertains as a thinking individual.

3.3

One gets further insight into Spinoza's thought on this point by considering the difference between his view and that of Descartes.

In dealing with the problem of error, Descartes held that error depends on the combination of two factors in the human mind, namely, the power of knowing or understanding, and the power of choice or free will. Error, he believed, was the consequence of an interrelation between these two faculties of the mind. His contention was that through the faculty of understanding we merely apprehend or grasp ideas but do not affirm or deny anything. The faculty of the will, on the other hand, merely affirms or denies what is presented to the intellect or the understanding. "The faculty of will," as he says in the *Fourth Meditation,* "consists solely in our having the power of choosing to do a thing or choosing not to do it (that is, to affirm or deny, to pursue or shun it), or rather it consists solely in the fact that in order to affirm or deny, pursue or shun those things placed before us by the understanding, we act so that we are unconscious that any outside force constrains us in doing so." Error is caused, in his

---

[1]S. Hampshire, "Spinoza and the Idea of Freedom," *Proceedings of the British Academy,* Vol. XLVI 1960, pp. 195–215.

own words, "when the will which is of wider range than understanding, asserts something which I do not understand." It is, therefore, the failure to restrain the will within the limits of understanding that causes error.

This means that, for Descartes, freedom is involved not only in the act of affirmation or denial, but also when lack of adequate or certain knowledge induces the mind to withhold judgment and thus maintain the will in a condition of indifference with respect to its object. Spinoza disassociates himself from Descartes to the extent that he does "not admit that liberty which Descartes ascribes to the Mind" (*Ep* 12). On the other hand, he appears to suggest (in the same letter) that he endorses Descartes insofar as Descartes believed "that our liberty is placed . . . in the mode of assertion or denial, so that *the less indifferently we affirm or deny something the more we are free*" (my italics). Spinoza's point is that if the state of indifference, as it consists in having the choice to affirm or deny, implies that in this state we do not possess certain knowledge, then clearly indifference is a sign of doubt, uncertainty, and inadequate knowledge. One may express the same thing by saying that we are more free when we have the certainty involved in adequate ideas than when we are in doubt or do not know. To say, therefore, that when we act upon certain knowledge we necessarily act freely, does not mean, nor does it entail, that because we act necessarily we are not acting freely. For Spinoza 'necessity' and 'freedom', in the sense involved here, are not incompatible notions. We are never more free, Spinoza would hold, than when we affirm something in the way that we affirm that it necessarily follows, from the nature of a Euclidean triangle, for its three angles to be equal to two right angles. Such a necessity is the sort involved in understanding the true nature of triangles. To affirm in this manner is to have ideas of thought-objects correlative with the nature of things as they are. If and when we do not have this kind of knowledge, our affirmation or action does not have the necessity which follows from certain knowledge. So that even though we may feel free to affirm or deny something that we are not certain is true, the action or affirmation accompanying such a state of mind is not and cannot be of the kind which follows from a distinct and clear perception.

In other words, while Descartes claims that "we are free not only when our ignorance of right renders us indifferent, but also . . . when a clear perception impels us to prosecute some definite course" (Descartes' reply to VI Objection, Item 6), Spinoza's view is that even if it makes sense to speak of the will having a wider range than understanding, it cannot mean that an action that is correlated with confused and inadequate perception or understanding is free in the same sense as when it is correlated with adequate perception. The freedom or liberty involved in being aware of having the ability to affirm or deny something we do not fully understand, or in acting without comprehending all the relevant conditions which explain our choice, is not and cannot be of the kind that is involved in our understanding the impossiblity of there being an alternative to what must be affirmed if we are to have true knowledge, and our act correlative to it is to be rational and free. Freedom which corresponds, in other words, to inadequate ideas or confused understanding, is not that which corresponds to adequate ideas and clear understanding. It would be very odd, Spinoza would say, if someone were to claim that he is free insofar as he can disagree, or refuse to believe that the three angles of a Euclidean triange are equal to two right angles. A person's claim to such freedom is only an indication of his failure to understand the nature of the facts involved in the conception of a triangle. Error, for Spinoza, consists not, as Descartes believed, in the affirmation by the will of something which is beyond the range of understanding, but "solely in the privation which mutilated and confused ideas involve" (*E* II, 49 S).

Spinoza, of course, must not be taken to deny that there is a sense in which it is possible for a man to believe and act so that he *feels* certain of the truth of the affirmation while it may, in fact, be false. As noted in the last chapter, there is a difference between the psychological certainty about the truth of an idea and the certainty of knowledge involved in an adequate and true idea. Spinoza's position is that, in the case of mere psychological certainty, we may say only that a man does not doubt, but we cannot properly say that he is certain. To believe or assent to something because one has no doubt about its truth, is quite different from believing something because one is certain about its truth. To say that one does not doubt is only to imply that there are no causes sufficient to alter one's imagination; whereas 'certitude' is to be understood as something positive, and not a mere absence of doubt. Hence, 'privation of certitude', which is the same as 'not to have doubt', amounts, for Spinoza, to falsity (*E* II, 49S). On the basis of these distinctions, Spinoza believes that falsity and error consist in inadequate perception and not, as Descartes believed, in affirmation by the will of something which is beyond understanding. Descartes takes 'the will' and 'the understanding' to be distinct; for Spinoza the two are one and the same.

Spinoza has reasons for not making a distinction between the intellect and the will. Spinoza's theory of ideas involves acceptance of the fact that any form of mental activity ascribable to an individual or anything which can be described by a mental predicate in relation to him, is a mode of thought. And all modes of thought are ideas in the most general sense of the word 'idea'. When we describe anything as an instance of willing, it is an instance of either believing or disbelieving, desiring or avoiding, affirming or negating, something. These are ways in which we perceive the world as it affects us as psycho-physical organisms. There is no 'faculty' apart from, or over and above, such individual volitions or ideas, which does the willing or thinking. Mind is not an entity distinct from the ideas that we ascribe to it. The human mind or intellect is identical with the ideas of various sorts that are entertained by an individual as a person. And since all mental acts are 'ideas', there is no seperate and distinguishable category to which conceptions, perceptions, imaginings, volitions, and so forth, can each be said to belong. The only distinctions between ideas is the one between ideas which are adequate and/or true, and those which are inadequate and/or false. Hence Spinoza's statement that "the will and intellect are nothing but the individual volitions and ideas themselves. But the in dividual volition and the idea are one and the same. Therefore the will and intellect are one and the same" (*E* II, 49 Dem). The will or intellect, considered as faculties, are only abstractions. They are related to this or that particular idea or volition in the same way, Spinoza points out, as, for instance, rockiness is related to this or that rock, or humanity is related to this or that man (*E* II, 48S). They are what he calls, 'things of reason' (*entia rationis*), and not real things (*ST* II 15 and *Ep* 2). Therefore, he maintains, that even to ask the question whether the will is free is entirely unnecessary and highly misleading.[2]

---

[2]This observation of Spinoza's can be understood a little more clearly by reference to the distinction that he draws between 'ideas', 'images', and 'words' in *E* II 49S (see also *DIE* 88 and 89). He points out that it is the confusion involved in our minds about the nature of the above three things, and the lack of sufficient accuracy and care in distinguishing them, that creates such ignorance about the doctrine of free will, the proper understanding of which, he thinks, is so essential both to philosophical speculation and the wise conduct of life.

To entertain an idea is to affirm or deny something. Individual acts of willing, thinking, desiring or believing, are individual acts of affirmation or denial. To say that we choose this or that is no more than to say we accept, agree, believe or decide this or that. No matter what the mode of Thought may be, there is always in principle an answer to the question "why did one accept, believe or decide whatever one did?" There are always necessary and sufficient conditions which explain that particular mode of Thought, even though no one may, in fact, be able to give an acount of those conditions. Insofar as individual acts of affirmation or denial are explainable by reference to conditions involving other modes of Thought, any specific act of will or choice is a determinate mode of Thought. To say that it is 'determined' is no more than to say that there is, in principle, an explanation for it.

3.4

An individual volition, an idea in a human mind, is the consequent of man's essence or nature, as expressed through his tendency to self-assertion as an individual having a mind. His tendency to self-assertion as an individual having a body is the necessary consequent of the causal conditions pertaining to his nature as a mode of extension. The mental aspect of *conatus* has

---

Ideas as *conceptions* of the mind are not the same thing as *images* which are formed in us by our contact with the external world. Nor is an idea as a conception of the mind to be confused with the *words* used to express it. From this view it would also seem to follow that if we understand by 'a proposition', 'an expression of thought in language', and hold that only propositions can be true or false, Spinoza would not agree with us. For his 'idea', clearly, is not a proposition in this sense, and yet it can be true or false, adequate or inadequate.

no causal connection with the body, nor does the physical aspect of *conatus* causally determine the mind. There is a sense, then, in which a volition or mode of Thought cannot be the cause of any changes or movement of the body. For the 'causal' conditions which explain modes of Thought must be other modes of Thought, and not modes of Extension. An idea is not a physical entity nor a physical entity an idea. The question of why I believe what I believe, choose, decide, desire, or think what I do, must properly be answered in terms of certain other beliefs, thoughts, decisions, choices and desires that I entertain, each of which are modes of Thought or ideas and belong to the same category, namely, Thought. The question "why do any particular movements in and of my body occur?" must properly be answered in terms of certain other movements in and of my body, all of which, being modes of Extension, have something in common with one another and, therefore, can also be understood and explained through one another (*E* I, A5 & 4). One's desires and decisions cannot be said to cause the movement of one's body any more than the body can be said to cause the mind to think (*E* III, 2 Dem. & S). But since the human mind is the idea itself or knowledge of the human body (*E* II, 19 Dem.), the human mind is inseparable from the human body. That is to say, our awareness of ourselves or of objects in our enviornment is mediated through our own bodies, and our ideas of other things are ideas of their effects upon our own bodies.[3] Even the ideas we entertain that do not involve direct contact with, or indirect influence of, other bodies upon our own bodies involve complicated cor-

---

[3]See Errol E. Harris, *Salvation From Despair: A Reappraisal of Spinoza's Philosophy* (The Hague, Martinus Nijhoff, 1973), pp. 81–82, for a lucid and insightful explanation of Spinoza's statement "The human mind is the idea itself or knowledge of the human body."

relative modifications occurring within our bodies. But the mind, or ideas in the human mind, and the body or modification of the human body, exist simultaneously, without one being the *cause* of the changes in the other. This is Spinoza's theory which is generally described as 'parallelism'. Because of this view, commentators like H.H. Joachim have been led to remark that Spinoza makes "the last vestiges of the popular conception of freewill disappear,"[4] as though to say, what a tragedy that he should be so profoundly misguided.

This charge, incidentally, is not of much philosophical significance in itself. What is significant and worth looking into are the grounds upon which it is founded. An examination of these grounds is important to an understanding of Spinoza's concept of desire and its relation to human action.

Joachim's contention is that Spinoza's conception, or rather misconception, of desire, or *cupidatis,* is responsible for his polemic against freedom of the will. What Spinoza does, as Joachim puts it, "is to admit the fact of conscious desire whilst denying the reality of purposive action"[5]. It would indeed be difficult to deny that there are some grounds for believing that this is what Spinoza is engaged in doing. Take, for instance, Spinoza's statement "There is no difference between appetite and desire, unless in this particular, that desire is generally related to men insofar as they are conscious of their appetites, and it may therefore be defined as appetite of which they are conscious" (*E* III, 9S); and "whether a man be conscious of his appetite or not the appetite itself remains one and the same" (*E* III, Aff. Def. 1, Expl.). These statements do give an impression that since appetite, for

[4]H.H. Joachim, *A Study of the Ethics of Spinoza* (Oxford, Clarendon Press, 1901), p. 198.

[5]Ibid., p. 228

Spinoza, is the *conatus* of man in the form of a blind striving, instinctive impulse or drive for self-preservation, and desire is merely consciousness of this striving, then whether a human being acts instinctively and without knowing what he is doing, or intentionally, deliberately and with a conscious purpose in mind, makes no difference as to what, in fact, he does or would do. It seems that, for Spinoza, man is no different from any other animate or inanimate thing, as we ordinarilly distinguish them, insofar as his behavior is unavoidably conditioned or determined by his appetitive nature. Man is a creature who is also at times conscious of his drives, impulses and strivings; this consciousness, however, does not make any difference to his behavior, because consciousness of appetite does not make the slightest alteration in the appetites themselves. So whether a person is conscious of his appetites or not, his behavior would be one and the same. Man is a helpless creature in the hands of fate, like clay in the hands of a potter, and there is no way in which he can consciously control his behavior.

We also find, however, that Spinoza strongly repudiates the charge that he reduces man to the level of plants or stones (see *Ep* 21), and he adds that whoever believes him to hold such a view "has thoroughly misunderstood my meaning." Spinoza, evidently, was not unaware that his thought was liable to this kind of misunderstanding. But since this usual interpretation imputes to him a view which he vehemently rejects, it must be possible to understand his thought in a way that reveals what, in fact, he did mean.

Joachim's view on this issue can be taken as a standard, since much misunderstanding of Spinoza, tradiitionally, is of the kind reflected in Joachim's commentary. He observes that the purposive action which Spinoza discredits and contemptuously rejects, is action towards "ideals not yet real, but to be realized," or "action with a view to the attainment of an unpossessed 'better'."[6]

As a start, in reading the treatise, *On the Improvement of the Understanding,* one cannot fail to notice Spinoza's autobiographical statements in the first few pages which contain the following expressions: "I finally resolved to enquire . . . "; "I seriously devoted myself to the search for something different and new . . . "; "with this end in view I made many efforts"; "I forced myself to seek with all my strength . . . "; "Love towards a thing eternal is greatly to be desired and sought for with all our strength"; "Man conceives of a character much more stable than his own, . . . and sees that there is no reason why he should not himself acquire such a character. This is the end for which I strive; to attain such character myself and to endeavor that many should attain it with me." There is also at least one passage in his correspondence that not only recognizes but recommends conscious purposeful action. In this letter (*Ep* 37), Spinoza answers a question from Bouwmeester, who requested to know the method by which one may proceed in the search for the highest knowledge. After outlining the method consisting, essentially, of entertaining adequate and true ideas, Spinoza warns him "that for all these there are required incessant thought and a most constant mind and purpose. To gain these, it is first of all necessary to adopt a definite mode and plan of life, and to set before one a definite end." These remarks could hardly come from a man who is denying "action with a view to the attainment of an un-

---

[6]Ibid., p. 232. Joachim is not the only one to hold such a view. See also, W.G. DeBurgh, "Spinoza", *Philosophy* 11, 1936, pp. 271-288; Rapheal Demos in "Spinoza's Doctrine of Privation," *Philosophy* 8, 1933, pp. 155-166, A.E. Taylor in "Some Incoherencies in Spinozism," *Mind* 46, 1927, pp. 281-301, to name a few, express the same attitude as Joachim's.

possessed better", or form one who was rejecting purposive action, or action with an end in view, or action towards acquiring a certain character which one considers as ideal.

It is not likely that Spinoza was unaware of the paradox involved in his holding two seemingly incompatible views, namely: (1) that every particular thing, as a finite mode, has a cause or explanation, and every effect is necessarily related to its explanatory conditions, and the existence of a finite mode must involve reference to determining conditions outside its own nature; and (2) that human beings can legitimately be said to direct their efforts knowingly, deliberately, and purposefully towards an end of which they are conscious.

It is more probably that he had in mind some argument to show that these two theses are not incompatible; that the understanding of a man's behavior by reference to the explanatory conditons does not preclude the applicability of the concept of purposive and intentional action. What he would doubtless have insisted is that any instance of human behavior regarded philosophically as a particular mode of God must in principle be completely explainable by reference to antecedent conditions, dependent ultimately upon the very nature of God or the original principle of the universe as it is. Since it makes no sense to talk of God or the primal reality itself acting with a purpose or end other than its own nature or essence, and since finite individuals are only modes existing and acting within the universe which derives its nature from the primal reality or God, there is a sense in which they can be said to be acting with a purpose which is part of them by virtue of the essential nature of God. So that what we ordinarily call 'purpose' in human beings is itself, *qua* a modification of God, a manifestation of the essential nature of God and determined by Him insofar as "He is manifested through the nature of the human mind" (*E* II, 11C).

The view that Spinoza makes use of the concept of conscious purpose while denying its applicability is based upon the argument that Spinoza's denial of conscious purpose in human beings is the consequence of his failure to distinguish between appetite and desire. Joachim develops his argument as follows: Spinoza has stated that consciousness of appetite leaves the appetite unmodified or unchanged. This implies that since "the end for the sake of which we do anything" is, according to Spinoza, nothing but appeitie (*E* IV, Df, 7), then the end or purpose of which we are conscious is the end for which we would have acted anyway, whether we were conscious of it or not.[7] Now, even admitting that Sinoza's statements give some grounds for this interpretation, it is impossible to ignore the fact that he does not merely use the notion of conscious purpose, but recognizes it as an essential part of man's nature, in carefully distinguishing between appetite and desire. Spinoza's definition of desire is very elusive and his concept of it, therefore, is not easy to understand. An adequate analysis of this concept is crucial to understanding his philosophy of mind and his concept of action.

3.5

Before we examine his notion of 'desire', however, there is one point that may be important to raise. When we read Spinoza's statement in his treatise *On the Improvement of the Understanding,* "Man conceives a human character much more stable than his own, and sees that there is no reason why he should not himself acquire such a character," there arises a question about the nature of this conception. The question is whether the conception of a

---

[7]Cf. C.D. Broad, *Five Types of Ethical Theory* (London: Routledge and Kegan Paul, 1948), p. 24. Broad interprets, or rather misinterprets, Spinoza in the same manner as Joachim.

character more stable than one's own is formed at the level of knowledge described by Spinoza as 'imagination', or at the level of 'reason', or 'intuitive Knowledge'. If it is the expression of reason or intuitive knowledge, then it appears that a man would have already attained the level of knowledge to which he was aspiring; this seems unlikely if not absurd. If, however, this conception is formed at the level described by Spinoza as "the first kind of knowledge" (*E* II, 40 S2), which seems to be the only alternative left, then it implies that, at the level of *imagination,* one can legitimately be said to act with a conscious end in view; hence purposive activity becomes acceptable at this level. Furthermore, such purposive activity must be logically necessary in the process to advance to the stage of action which follows from, or is correlated with, knowledge based on reason. To seek the means to realize an ideal that is presented in the imagination undeniably involves consciously directed effort. Spinoza never denied that it was possible for man to discover an ideal as an end and to find the means to attain it. He admits without ambiguity that he wishes "to direct all sciences to one end and aim, so that we may attain to the supreme human perfection. . . . All our actions and thoughts must be directed to this end" (*DIE* 16).

He even lays down some provisional rules of behavior while the search for the means of improvement and purification of understanding is in progress (*DIE* 17). It is interesting and important to note that these rules are offered as preliminary prescriptions, and not as mere descriptions of the way to attain 'the end'. The question Spinoza seeks to answer in his philosophy is, indeed, "what shall I do to inherit eternal life?" It is sometimes suggested that Spinoza's answer to this is "not a command; the *Ethics* contains no 'oughts', no imperatives, only 'eternal truth'."[8]

---

[8]See A.G. Wernham, *Spinoza's Political Works* (Oxford, Clarendon Press,

However, to accept that Spinoza tried to give human beings a clear and distinct understanding of themselves and their emotions—so that he who has this also has 'love of God' and 'salvation'—and to deny that the context in which these statements are made is a context which allows one to prescribe what to do in order to attain the end, would be to miss the point of Spinoza's *Ethics,* for there is no doubt that Spinoza's aim was ethical, namely, to guide human action. How can one reasonably argue, then, that Spinoza's statements have no prescriptive content and yet be guided by them? In pointing out eternal truths, he is also suggesting (by conversational implicature, at least) that those who understand them will, at the same time, make an effort to attain the end. It does not seem plausible that Spinoza merely describes what is supremely good, and shows us the method by which to attain it, without the explicit suggestion or assumption that man should, in the prescriptive sense, aim at attaining it.

3.6

To return to the distinction between desire and appetite; we have seen that 'will' *(voluntas),* 'appetite' *(appetitus)* and 'desire' *(cupiditas)* are taken by Spinoza as related notions. They are parts of man's striving for self-preservation or *conatus.* Such striving constitutes the very essence or nature of man. To speak of being free

---

1958), pp. 10 and 20. (Professor Alan Donagan also appears to hold a view similar to Wernham's in an as yet unpublished paper.) Mr. Wernam seems to have overlooked the implications of the provisional rules of life offered by Spinoza in *DIE*, as well as the following paragraph in *Ep* 43 (1671) in which Spinoza says "It is false to assert that I maintain that there is no room left for precepts or commands or . . . that there is no expectation of reward or punishment since everything is affirmed to proceed from God by inexorable necessity."

in this 'striving', as though one had the power either to strive or not to strive to preserve oneself, is meaningless. Every form of human activity, no matter how self-destructive it may be, manifests this striving. A human being cannot free himself from this striving without ceasing to be alive. In one sense, his individuality consists in the manifestation of his *conatus.*

Now, as human beings, we naturally strive for certain things such as pleasures, and avoid others, such as pains. Those which we strive for are generally described by us as 'good', and those we avoid are called 'bad' or 'evil'. From this follows Spinoza's well-known and highly controversial statement, "We neither strive for, wish, seek nor desire anything because we think it to be good, but on the contrary, we adjudge a thing to be good because we strive for, wish, seek or desire it" (*E* III, 9S). The significance of this passage is generally somewhat distorted. Spinoza does not, and cannot, mean that whenever a human being seeks, strives, or wishes to have or do anything, it becomes good by the mere fact that he desires it. Nor does he mean that anything whatever that man at any time in fact desires is always good. He is not, as far as I can see, putting forward any implausible or absurd theory in his statement. What he means is that man's desires, which find expression in an inclination and disinclination toward various things, play a decisive role in his recognition and description of things as good or bad. He is suggesting that it is a necessary truth, considering the nature of man, that a thing could not be described as 'good' if no individual were ever disposed or inclined or attracted toward it in some sense; or, as Spinoza would put it, if there were no individual with whose nature the thing described as good agrees (*E* IV, 31 Dem and C). It seems fairly plain that things which are ordinarily considered and described as 'good', such as knowledge or peace of mind, must in fact have been desired by man at some stage of human history before they came to be looked upon as worthy of being sought. With successive advancement in conceptual ability, together with intellectual, social and moral sophistication, human beings have learned to seek things which are generally considered to be good, even though they are not necessarily desired or sought after by everyone.

Our beliefs about things which are good or bad are constantly changing. Spinoza was certainly right in recognizing that man's description of things as good or evil, in general, depends upon the changes in his desires, which result from changes in man's perception of the world and of himself. This would also explain the difference in value attached to similar things in different societies at the same time, and in the same society at different times.

The implications of the alleged lack of distinction between desire and appetite in Spinoza's thought are that it makes no sense to say we desire something which we consciously recognize as good. From this standpoint it becomes possible to understand Spinoza as arguing that conscious desire for something presupposes unconscious desire (in an even more genuine sense of 'unconscious' than is given by 'propensity', or 'disposition') from which the conscious desire arises. Since Spinoza's notion of 'appetite' seems to comprehend all the potential urges of man to desire things, he is interpreted as saying that when a man consciously desires a thing, all that happens is that appetites, which form the essential part of him, come to the level of consciousness. A man does not consciously seek anything different from what he has a potential capacity or disposition to desire. Since appetite, or 'desire of which a man is *un*conscious' is, for Spinoza, identical with 'desire of which a man is conscious', namely, *cupiditas,* he is believed to be stating a tautology. Thus he would be holding the view that since unconscious desire is the same as conscious desire, the words 'conscious' and 'unconscious' are interchangeable in this context. One must admit that if Spinoza is maintaining such a view in explaining the nature of desire, then there is perhaps no way of avoiding the conclusion that consciousness of appetite makes no difference in what a man does or would do.

The important point to be taken into account here is that Spinoza's view, that for a person to have a desire is for him to be conscious of appetite, does not entail, nor is it meant by him to imply (in any sense of 'imply') that the behavior which accompanies or results from a man's state of consciously desiring something is qualitatively identical with that which would follow from his (nonconscious) appetite. Contrary to the commonly accepted view, Spinoza does in fact recognize the difference between desire and appetite; he makes a definite point of clarifying his position in order to avoid being misunderstood in the fashion in which he has been misunderstood.

The distinctions which he makes in *E* III, Aff. Def. 1 and in *E*III 56 Dem., are extremely important in this respect. In the explanation to *E* III, Aff. Def. 1, Spinoza seems to apologize for appearing to be guilty of tautology in his earlier definition of desire (*E* III, 9S). He warns us significantly, "I have not explained desire by appetite," and he adds that if he had explained desire by appetite, then he would have had to say that "desire is the essence itself of man insofar as it is considered as determined to any action." That is, he would have had to say that explanations of an action by reference to appetite or to desire are one and the same (qualitatively). Evidently, however, he is not prepared to say that; for he explains that if he had held such a view of the nature of desire, then it would not be possible for him to maintain that "The mind does not know itself except insofar as it perceives the ideas of the affections of the body" (*E* II, 23). Now for the mind to know itself is to have an idea of an idea. The difference between being merely 'conscious' and being 'self-conscious' consists in this: to be conscious is to have an idea correlative to the modifications or affections of the body; but to be *self*-conscious is to be conscious of an idea correlative with the affections of the body; that is, to have an idea of an idea.

In this sense self-consciousness is, by its nature, reflexive. I can be aware of a thing without being aware that I am aware of it. A feeling of discomfort on the bridge of my nose, for instance, may simultaneously and unreflectively be accompanied by a movement of my hand to remove my glasses. I may, on the other hand, experience such a feeling of discomfort and sit for awhile, being aware of this feeling, wondering whether or not to remove my glasses, and may eventually remove them. There is clearly a difference between these two cases. In the first case, I cannot say that I *desired* to remove my glasses, for I was not even aware that I was removing them. In the second case, I was aware of what I wanted to do, namely, to remove the feeling of discomfort; I knew I could achieve this by removing the glasses, and decided to do so. One is conscious activity, the other is self-conscious. Self-consciousness involves being conscious, but being conscious does not imply being self-conscious. The distinction Spinoza tries to make is precisely between activity which is self-conscious and that which is not. Appetitive behavior is conscious behavior, but behavior explainable in terms of desire is self-conscious behavior. There is a qualitative distinction between the two which cannot be ignored if one is to give a coherent account of human action.

Spinoza's explanation seems to be that consciousness, which is correlated with the affections of one's body, involves being conscious of the effects of the external world upon one's body, and this includes a perceptual knowledge of the circumstances in the situation. So, in the absence of consciousness correlative with his body's affections, a human being will not be in a position to be self-conscious, nor will it be possible for him to have a desire; hence, no determinate action can follow. That is to say, the presence of desires in man logically presupposes that his body be affected by certain objects in the empirical world. This, of course, does not mean that if a man's body is affected by certain objects in the empirical world then certain desires are necessarily experienced by him. The affections or changes in the body implied in the experience of desire presuppose the presence of appetites without which an individual will not be regarded as a *person.* Spinoza maintains that in the absence of desire a person will not be, as he puts it, "determined toward any action." What he means is that the difference between desire and appetite consists in the fact that desire implies a self-conscious cognitive state, in which the behavior of a human being is governed by the consciousness of an end or a goal which he deliberately attempts to achieve through the exercise of his desires. These desires, he acknowledges (*E* III, 56 Dem.), can vary, just as consciousness of an end can vary, according to a man's changing dispositions and the kind of objects by which he is affected.

3.7

The crucial question which arises now is whether the qualitative distinction between desire and appetite permits one to conclude that when we desire something and act to fulfill that desire, the bodily movement involved is *caused* by the desire. Spinoza's answer to this is that "The body cannot determine the mind to thought, neither can the mind determine the body to motion nor rest . . . " (*E* III, 2). Unless I am mistaken, this statement is the first of its kind in so-called modern philosophy which suggests a distinction between causes and reasons of human behavior, and it also sheds much needed light on the notion of intentional action.

Let us consider the latter point first, namely, the notion of 'intentional action'. What exactly is it that Spinoza wishes to deny here? What kind of interaction between mind and body is being ruled out by the above statement, and what kind of interaction is not? On the fact of it, it seems that Spinoza is ruling out the possibility of any influence of the body on the mind and of the mind on the body. This is unlikely; for if, as he maintains, the human mind is the idea of the human body (*E* II, 19 Dm), then nothing can count as an idea in a person's mind without correlative physical modifications occurring in that person's body. Furthermore, since the order and connection of (true) ideas is the same as the order and connection of things, a true idea of the nature of the mind will be necessarily related to the mind (as it really is), and when this is truly understood it would be found that what we call the 'mind' is necessarily related to the body, for a human being or a person is composed of both mind and body; he is a 'union of mind and body'. To understand this union is to grasp the truth that our conception of the mind cannot be a true conception without perceiving that it is necessarily related to the body; to grasp this is to understand "what should be understood by the union of mind and body." The changes in the body are indeed causally related to other changes in the body as caused by external bodies. The correlative ideas in the mind are logically related to other ideas corresponding to the causal counterparts of the modification of the body. What Spinoza denies, and rightly so, is the *causal* relation between the mind and the body. But to deny this is not to say that there is no relation of any kind between the mind and the body—especailly since, throughtout, Spinoza emphasizes that the human mind is *inseparable* from the human body.

How can the two be inseparable and yet be wholly unrelated? Surely *causal* relation is not the only kind of relation that can exist between the two. It is difficult to understand the obsessive concern over the *causal* relation between mind and body in the history of philosophical thought. As a matter of fact, Spinoza admits that what happens in a person's body does affect his mind, and what happens in his mind does affect his body. His explanation in the *Short Treatise,* of how consumption of wine by a person can banish his sorrow, recognizes this much.

In Chapter 20 of the *Short Treatise* II Spinoza answers some objections raised about casual relation between mind and body, and offers some examples of the kind of thing that may be said against his stand. If it is the case, the objector says to him, that the body cannot affect the mind, then how is it that when we are feeling sorrowful, drinking wine affects the mind and helps alleviate or revome depressive mental state?

Spinoza's answer is interesting as well as instructive. He starts by saying that we must make a distinction between man's awareness which is correlated with the changes in his body, which constitutes his awareness of his body, and the judgment that he comes to make as to whether what he experiences is good or bad, pleasant or unpleasant. The latter is an idea of the idea of the body and not simply an idea of the body. For a person to be in a state of sorrow, he must be aware of the loss of something judged to be good. A man's sorrow is caused, Spinoza explains, by the thought that the loss of good that he is aware of will bring about evil. Correlative to and simultaneously with this thought or idea in his mind, certain changes within his body are necessarily taking place. Drinking of wine (or taking a drug) affects the change in the proportion of movement of the physical parts within the body, correlative to which, the ideas also are modified. It is not the case that the wine affects the mind, but that the wine affects the body, and correlative to these modifications the idea (of loss of good) is modified through diversion of the thought of evil.

The upshot of this does not become fully clear until we ask

Spinoza for an answer to the questions: (1) Can my mind affect my own body? and (2) Can I intentionally move my body in the sense in which I may desire something and deliberately move my body to satisfy that desire? Spinoza's answer to both these questions seems to be 'yes'. For since the mind of each person is the idea of his own body—and we have seen already what that means—Peter's mind, say, which is the idea of Peter's own body, can well move Peter's body but it cannot move Paul's body, which can be moved only by the mind constituted of the idea of Paul's body (*ST* II 20).

In other words, Spinoza maintains that the sense in which I can intentionally move my own arm is the sense in which I cannot intentionally move your arm; for the idea of my own body is united to my body in a way it is not, and cannot be, related to a body other than my own. I cannot, for instance, meaningfully be said to intend to move your arm up. I can, however, by intentionally moving my body or my arm, make contact with your body and lift your arm up. In that case, you cannot be said to be intentionally moving your arm up. Suppose that I order or request that you lift up your arm, as a result of which you raise your arm. In this case, again, I cannot be said to have intentionally raised your arm, but only to have intentionally made the movements of my body which amounted to the production of the sound that counted as an order or request for you to raise your arm. There is clearly no causal connection nor a logical one between my ordering you to raise your arm and your arm going up. Only you could raise your arm intentionally. I cannot move it intentionally; for my mind is united to my body, and your mind is united to your own. Of course, every individual human being's body can be influenced by his own mind, and Spinoza does not wish to deny this; but the sense in which a person's own body is influenced by his own mind is not and cannot be the way in which a person's body can be influenced by a mind that is united with a body other than his own. This may well be part of what Spinoza was thinking when he denied that the mind determines the body and the body determines the mind: "When a stone lies still," he says (*ST* II 19), "then it is impossible that it should be moved by the power of thought," but it may be moved, for example, by "another stone, having greater motion than this has rest." In other words, he suggests that it does not make sense for me to say that I am intentionally lifting the weights or driving the car. Or, if I do say this, it is only in a derivative or secondary sense of intentionally. Strictly speaking, the notion of intentionality is applicable only with respect to certain movements of one's own body or parts of one's body, but not with respect to anything else. Hence, the model for explaining externally directed intentional action, Spinoza would hold, is an inappropriate model to explain the relation between one's own mind and body.

3.8

Let us now examine, Spinoza's distinction between causes and reasons.

Spinoza holds that "Man is composed of mind and body" (*E* II, 13 C). It is logically impossible to attribute an idea to a man's mind without implying some correlative physical changes occurring in his body. Ideas in the human mind, however, can be explained only by reference to other ideas as their causes or reasons; and finite modes of Extension are causally explainable only by reference to other finite modes of Extension (*E* I, 28). The reason for this is that "things which have nothing mutually in common with one another cannot through one another be mutually understood" (*E* I, A5). The order and connection of ideas being the same, however, as the order and connection of things (*E* II, 7) implies that there cannnot be an idea in the human mind without correlative affections of the body.

Now, since all mental activities predicable of a human being are also modes of Thought, to say that a man 'willed' something is the same as to say that he desired, affirmed, believed, or assented to something. To will or desire something is for a person to be conscious of an idea. Since consciousness itself is a mode of Thought or an 'idea', then, when I 'will' something, I have an idea of an idea. Corresponding to this idea there is necessarily a mode of Extension in the form of modification occurring in my body. In experiencing a desire, however, I am unaware of the affections or modifications in my body. So that in desiring something, we are not, nor need to be, conscious of the bodily affections, though the affections of the body are a necessary condition in any given instance of desiring or willing. This being the case, there may be a plausible explanation for statements of the form "I desire such and such", so that my action following the desire is considered to be the consequence of that desire and regarded as its explanatory condition.

In claiming that the movement of my body, involved in my action, was caused by my desire for a specific end, I cannot possibly be implying a denial of the existence of a mode or modes of Extension correlative to my desire. Any instance of desire, as a mode of Thought, must ultimately involve reference to an identifiable person as a mode of Extension, and to certain physical changes occurring within his body which are also modes of Extension. What I am claiming, in referring to my desire to explain my action that involves bodily movement, is that, in being conscious of the desire, I am not directly conscious of the extensional correlates of this desire; these are causally connected with the changes occurring in my body. So when I say that "my action was determined by my desire," the actual efficient cause of the movement in and of my body can only be another modification of my body as a mode of Extension. For an explanation in terms of causal conditions for the movement of my body can (logically) be provided only by reference to other modes of the same category. But in being conscious of my desire (i.e., in having an idea of an idea) the *ideatum* or the object is not an affection of the body but another idea, as a thought-object. Since, in behaving purposefully, bodily movement necessarily accompanies conscious desire, the latter is perceived, believed, or in Spinoza's terms, 'imagined', to be the cause of the body's motion. To say, maintain, or believe, however, that my desire is the causal source of my body's motion is only an elliptical way of giving expression to the fact that the extensional correlate of desire is the causal source of motion in the body. The reason we tend to ignore reference to the extensional correlate of desire in explaining an intentional action is that, in the context of such behavior, it is the idea of conscious end that is significant. Although our body does move *because* of our desire, this is not a 'because' of causal connection, but of correlation of a different kind that Spinoza would call 'indirect cause' (see *ST* II 20, last paragraph), and to which he draws our attention by insisting on the impossibility of a causal connection between two modes belonging to different categories or attributes.

When one is asked "why did you do what you did?" the answer—if the action is regarded as voluntary, and in that sense intentional—is not provided by referring to a series of causal connections in the modes of Extension, or to the external and internal movements of the body. It is not these, but the conscious *reasons* for believing or desiring which accompany bodily movement that are relevant in the context of intentional behavior. Spinoza's view would clearly seem to be that reasons for actions cannot be identified with causes for actions, for he recognizes that Extension and Thought are distinct attributes, each infinite in its own kind and hence independent of the other. Modes of one attribute, therefore, are not reducible to the modes of another. The causal explanation of a mode of Extension can be given (and this is, again, a logical 'can') only by reference to modes belonging to the same category. One idea, be it a belief, a desire, a judgment or any other aspect of mind, can be explained only by reference to other ideas, such as beliefs, desires, or judgments.

Spinoza does seem to hold that the connecting link between a series of ideas, too, is causal; but, as explained earlier, he cannot be using the term 'causal' in the same sense as one that refers to the relation between modes of Extension. One billiard ball, as a physical object can hit another billiard ball and push it, thus *causing it to move as a physical object.* However, beliefs, judgments, decisions, and desires are not the kinds of things about which it makes sense to say that one belief or judgment was hit by another and pushed it, causing it to move, as though they were physical entities. This is the distinction that Spinoza suggests by differentiating between modes of Thought and modes of Extension. The relation among modes of Thought is indeed a necessary relation in the sense of 'logical', but not necessary in the sense of 'causal' that applies to the relation among modes of Extension.

It remains to be seen how 'reason' fits into this scheme. Spinoza's view seems to be that to attempt to explain human behavior by reference to conscious desires is to provide an answer to the question "why did you do what you did?" in terms of one's reasons for doing it. The provision for adequate reasons for an action is made by him to be the very condition of rational behavior. The explanation of man's behavior by reference to conscious desires, that is, reasons, is analogous to, but not identical with, the explanation of man's bodily movements by reference to the antecedent modes of Extension. Thus reasons function as sufficient conditions of conscious behavior. In this sense desires can be said to be efficient causes of actions.

Spinoza, in the Preface to *E* IV, accepts this. He also adds that although the desire to attain an end is to be accepted as the efficient cause of the existence of things, it is not to be construed as the final cause of their existence. By this, I think, Spinoza wishes to point out that the final cause of human behavior is always and invariably the appetite that forms the necessary part of the nature of man, as man. So that, in admitting desire as an efficient cause, Spinoza suggests that the final cause, namely appetite, is to be considered as the efficient cause of behavior in those circumstances in which a human being acts while being conscious or aware of the final cause. Since the final causes of behavior are appetites, rather than conscious desires, one's conscious desires, which are the efficient causes, are nothing other than appetites modified by consciousness. Therefore, to say that desire is only an efficient cause of man's behavior does not mean, nor does it imply, that desires are being deprived by Spinoza of the relevant kind of explanatory efficacy which must be ascribed to them in order for them to be regarded as the sufficient conditions for the existence of other affections of the mind and body.

Spinoza does not merely make use of the concept of purposeful and intentional action. He also admits—insofar as he accepts the possibility of improvement in man's understanding of his own nature, the nature of the world around him, and the nature of the very source and origin of things in the universe—that the effort to attain such knowledge, and conformity to action to it, cannot be explained adequately through reference to appetitive dispositions alone, but must necessarily involve the modification of appetites through one's consciousness of them.

Chapter Four

Cause

4.1

Spinoza expresses his conception of cause in statements of the following kind. God or substance is the cause of itself and of all things which exist in the universe (*E* I, 7 Dem. and *E* I, 25 S.); and every existing thing is in God and can neither be nor be conceived without him (*E* I, 15). God, therefore, is the universal, efficient, essential, first, principal, immanent, and proximate cause of all things (*E* I, 16, C1,2,3; *E* I, 18 and *E* I, 28 S.). Since there is no cause except the perfection and reality of God's nature which can explain his existence and his activity, God is also the free cause of all things (*E* I, 17 C2). These statements, couched in medieval terminology, are hard to follow as they stand. Even the most elaborate exposition of the sense of 'cause' involved here, the kind given, for instance, by H.A. Wolfson,[1] leaves one in the dark about the meaning of such statements.

But Despite the complexity of this list of causes it is not really as fanciful as it may at first appear. As Wolf correctly points out, "substitute 'conditions' for 'causes', and the classification still contains much that is true and valuable." He remarks that

> If by "cause" we mean "the totality of conditions," then there is no room for such elaborate classification of causes. But for all practical purposes we are satisfied to apply the term "cause" to something very far short of "the totality of conditions," and Mill has shown how arbitrary popular usage is in singling out now this, now that condition as "the cause," when, as a matter of fact, all the conditions are equally striking or interesting on different occasions of the same kind of occurrence.

Wolf suggests that it was according to this wider and looser use of the term that 'causes' were classified in such an elaborate way.[2]

I shall not be concerned here with each of the eight different senses of 'cause' mentioned in Spinoza's works but only with those which help to bring out its relevance to the concept of human action.

Spinoza understands a 'free cause' as that which is self-determined or self-explanatory (see *E* I, 17 Dem., C1 and C2). A

---

[1]See H.A. Wolfson, *The Philosophy of Spinoza* (Cambridge, Mass., 1934), Vol. I, Ch. IX.

[2]A. Wolf, *ST*, pp. 190–191. Wolf in his appended commentary to the *Short Treatise,* offers, in my view, a remarkably clear and concise account of the different senses of 'cause' in Spinoza by tracing them to Burgerdijck's *Logic*, London edition of 1651 (see *ST*, pp. 190–195, p. 179 and p. 188). Wolfson also refers to Burgerdijck for Spinoza's source of the eightfold classification. See Wolfson, *The Philosophy of Spinoza,* pp. 303–304.

thing that is caused to exist is a thing whose existence is explainable by reference to something other than itself or its own nature and constitution, and its existence is considered to be *causally necessary.* This sense of 'necessary' is distinct from, and almost opposed to, the sense of 'necessary' used to describe a thing that is self-determined, self-caused *(causa-sui)* and hence necessary through its own nature or through its essence. God's essence or essential nature is, for Spinoza, the ground or original source from which all things follow as a consequence. This is the same as saying that the existence of all things is, in the last analysis, explainable by reference to the nature of primal reality, or the principle of origin. It is in this sense that Spinoza regards everything as determined from the necessity of God's nature, or conditioned by God's nature, to exist and act in a certain manner (*E* I, 29).

One consequence of this view of causality is generally believed to be that the self-determination which makes it possible to describe God as 'free cause' of everything, seems to negate the contingency in the existence and nature of individual things or modes. If everything is what it is as the consequence of God's free causality, then every human action, being a mode of God, could not have been otherwise. If human action is no different from any other mode in this respect, then no distinction can be made between what happens as an event in the physical world, and what a man does as an agent. If everything is *causally* conditioned by the nature of God, over which a human being has no control or power whatever, then one cannot hold men responsible for what they do or for what is ascribed to them as their actions. Clearly, the notion of moral responsibility at least presupposes freedom of the sort which allows an exercise of choice and decision to human beings.

> As Hampshire points out, "If human action is shown to be deducible from a law of nature, that is, is exhibted as the effect of a cause, there is at least one sense in which we must say that the agent could not in this case have acted otherwise, or that no alternative action was possible; and if no alternative action was in this sense possible for him, it seems unreasonable to allow a sense to saying that he could have acted otherwise if he had chosen."[3]

Plausible as it might be to suggest that Spinoza's notion of causality implies such a view, I am inclined to believe, and shall try to show, that this attribution results from a serious misunderstanding of Spinoza's thought.

Spinoza recognizes that the context in which moral epithets and judgments can appropriately be applied to human beings and their actions is quite distinct from the one in which the concept of laws of nature is applicable. He would agree, for instance, that scientific laws of nature are descriptions of how things behave in the common order of nature, but they are not prescriptions as to how they ought to behave. He makes a distinction between natural or divine laws, and laws which are man made. The clearest expression of this distinction occurs in Chapter IV of his *Theologico-Political Treatise.* There he says that,

> The word "law", taken in the abstract, means that by which an individual or all things, or as many things as belong to a particular species, act in one and the same fixed and definite manner, which manner depends either on natural necessity or on human decree. A law which depends on natural necessity is one which necessarily follows from the nature, or from the definition of the thing in question; a law which depends on human

---

[3]S. Hampshire, *Spinoza* (Harmondsworth, Penguin, 1951), p. 150.

> decree . . . is one which men have laid down for themselves and others in order to live more safely or conveniently, or from some similar reason.

Spinoza offers laws of motion and laws of association as examples of laws of nature, but laws which men devise for the sake of maintaining social order or for some other convenience depend upon the power of the human mind. The perception of things as good or bad depends upon the principles devised by human beings, but things cannot be conceived as true or false without reference to the necessary laws of nature. His remark in this context, that "It is well to define and explain things by their proximate causes" (*TPT*, Ch. IV), is significant. It suggest that laws of nature function not as immediate or sufficient conditions, but only as remote or necessary conditions in the explanation of conscious human behavior. That is to say, human actions cannot be explained exclusively by reference to laws of nature. Apart from the fact that laws of nature are only remote conditions, we have, as he points out, no knowledge as to how the actual coordination and concatenation of things is brought about by them. Spinoza admits, therefore, that it is not only profitable or useful but necessary for right living to consider things as contingent (*TPT*, Ch. IV).

4.2

In considering the question of 'right living' for human beings, including conduct that can be judged as morally right or wrong, Spinoza would hold that it is logically necessary to consider things not in terms of laws of nature but in terms of principles of behavior recognized as being valid in the context of seeking and desiring certain ends. To say that a law of nature is universally valid is simply saying as Schlick rightly observes, that it holds in all cases where it is applicable.[4] Also, to say that such laws are 'necessary', as Spinoza does, is not to say that they compel things to behave in accordance with them. In the case of all living creatures, including human beings for instance, the principle of self-preservation is universally applicable. Surely this principle does not dictate how and in what specific ways human beings would act in order to preserve themselves. Granting the natural urge for self-preservation, which may legitimately be described as a law of nature, there is no evidence that Spinoza believed that human beings lack the requisite freedom to choose the most appropriate means of action to that end.

Spinoza recognized two logically distinct contexts of explanation of the existence of things. In the context of the laws of nature, everything is necessary in the sense that it follows from the essential nature of the primal principle or reality that is God. He seems to suggest that it is impossible, in this context, to say, without self-contradiction, that something could have been otherwise than it is. Spinoza maintains, however, that there is another context, within the system of nature and its universally applicable laws, in which laws are devised by human minds in order to seek a plan of living which serves to render life and state secure, and in which right living is made possible and moral conduct becomes relevant. It is in this context that the concepts of 'good' and 'evil' are of crucial importance and assume specific meaning: 'good' is that "which we certainly know is useful to us" (*E* IV, D1), and 'evil' is that "which we know hinders us from possessing anything that is good" (*E* IV, D2). The concepts of good and evil are, therefore, "modes of thought or notions

---

[4]M. Schlick, *Problems of Ethics* (New York: Prentice-Hall, 1939), Ch. VII.

which we form from comparison of one thing with another" (*E* IV, Pref.) in light of the ends that we consciously seek and desire. In order to live rightly, Spinoza holds, we must form an idea of man that can serve as a model of human nature and a standard of moral conduct, and provide us with a criterion for judging ourselves as well as other human beings. Any action that would prevent us from approximating that model would be 'evil'; and that which would serve as a means by which we may approach closer to it would be 'good'. The type of conduct attributable to this model or ideal of Spinoza's is evidently in accord with the principles or laws which must serve as a standard of conduct for human beings.

Had Spinoza categorically maintained that nothing whatsoever in a human being who strives to approach this ideal could possibly be otherwise than what has been predetermined or ordained for all time, and that there is no sense in saying that any human being at any time, in any context, is capable of acting otherwise than he does, then he would have been denying the freedom required to attribute moral responsibility to human beings. This denial would also seriously conflict with his ethical doctrines and his attempts to emancipate his fellow human beings from superstition and ignorance, and the hortatory character of his statements would be rendered completely inexplicable. It would not make sense for him to hope to bring about modification in the behavior and attitude of others if he held that no one could ever be otherwise than he is. Spinoza's plan or method for removal of ignorance is significant only if he accepts that it is genuinely possible to remove ignorance. Such a possibility must imply that under certain conditions, which he is himself capable of creating, a man can be otherwise than he would be in the absence of those conditions.

4.3

Spinoza's notion of causality is, perhaps, not as clear as one might wish, but the situation is not hopeless. There are a number of difficulties that arise mainly from the ambiguities in his use of the word 'cause' which we will now examine.

According to Spinoza, all modes express the nature of God in a determinate manner. That is to say, all modes are modes of one or the other attribute and, in this sense, the conception of an attribute of God is involved in all individual finite modes. Since modes are things which are 'in' something else (i.e., depend for their existence upon something other than their own nature), they must also be 'conceived' through that on which they depend. But there is a difficulty here. For Spinoza, to say that the 'conception' of an attribute of God is involved in all individual modes is the same as to say that God is the cause of every single mode. However, he also observes that "The idea of an individual thing actually existing has God for a cause, not insofar as He is infinite, but insofar as He is considered to be affected by another idea of an individual thing actually existing, of which idea also He is the cause insofar as He is affected by a third, and so on *ad infinitum,* (*E* II, 9). This, it shall be noted, is consistent with his statement that a finite thing having a determinate existence must have its cause of existence and action in another finite thing (*E* I, 28). Thus, he appears to accept that a finite mode needs, for the explanation of its existence, another finite mode as its cause. While accepting this he also goes on to say, for instance, that "without God nothing can be nor be conceived; for . . . God is the sole cause of the existence of all things" (*E* II, 10 S2). It is the addition of this latter statement that creates all the difficulties.

It is quite obvious that to say "individual things cannot be conceived without God, therefore *God is the cause of these things,*" is not the same as saying that "since an individual thing cannot exist unless so determined by another finite thing, then *one finite individual thing is the cause of existence of another finite individual thing.*" Spinoza uses the term 'cause' in these contexts, in clearly distinct senses; there is no reason to believe that he confuses one sense of the term with the other. In the first instance Spinoza evidently means that individual things logically involve the idea of God. The term 'conceive' is used in the sense of a logical relation between finite individual things and God, the principle of origin. Now if he were to mean that while a finite individual thing *can* be conceived without involving another finite thing as its 'cause', it can *not* be conceived without God, then one could argue that granting an individual thing cannot be conceived without God, it surely needs another finite thing to 'cause' it to exist. Since Spinoza insists that "An individual thing, or a thing which is finite and which has a determinate existence, cannot exist nor be determined to action unless it be determined to existence and action by another cause which is also finite and has a determinate existence" (*E* I, 28), and a finite mode for him is not identical with God or an attribute of God, he cannot be using the word 'cause' in exactly the same sense in both these contexts.

One may admit that a finite thing is a logical consequence of the nature of God, in the sense that the existence of a finite thing implies the conception of a reality that is *causa sui,* namely, God. It does not follow, however, that the essence of God, whatever it may be, is the 'cause' of the existence of finite things in the sense of 'cause' which implies not only the necessary but also the sufficient condition along with temporal sequence and change. Even if one grants that the conception of God or one of his attributes is a logically necessary condition for the essence and existence of an individual thing, Spinoza has not shown that this conception of God or his attributes also serves as the sufficient condition for the existence of a particular finite thing.

Spinoza sometimes uses another phrase to describe the relation between God and modes. The finite and determinate modes, he says, must "follow from God." In addition, the finite and determinate must "follow or be determined to existence by God or by some attribute of God, insofar as the attribute is modified by a modification which is finite and which has determinate existence" (*E* I, 28 Dem.). Once again the words 'follow' and 'be determined to existence' refer to the causal relation between finite things themselves, and not between finite things and God in His absolute nature. Spinoza does appear to maintain that to say" a finite thing as a determinate modification of God follows from another finite determinate mode" is the same as saying "a finite determinate mode follows from God." If he believed these statements were truly identical in meaning, then, first, he would ignore the distinction between necessary condition and sufficient condition in a causal relation, which he recognizes by distinguishing between 'remote' and 'proximate' cause; and second, he would disregard the distinction he makes between two kinds of existence. In *E* V, 29S, he points out that things can be conceived to exist with relation to a fixed time and place, or they can be conceived as eternal. This explanation suggests that the relation between that which is eternal and that which is not, is not of the same kind as the relation between things neither of which is eternal. This means that Spinoza must have in mind a distinction between the 'causal' relation that exists between God and finite individual things, and that which exists between finite individual things themselves.

4.4

The confusion over Spinoza's notion of 'cause' arises in part from his failure to distinguish clearly between the 'ground' and the 'cause' of the existence of finite things. To refer once again to *E* I, 28 and its Demonstration, where Spinoza holds that a finite thing cannot be produced by the absolute nature of any attribute of God, for if it were, it would be infinite and eternal. Therefore, a finite thing must be produced by another finite thing. Thus he tells us, for instance, that the cause of the existence of a human being is another human being (*E* I, 17S). When, therefore, Spinoza says that "God is the cause of the commencement of the existence of things and also of their continuance in existence" (*E* I, 24C), he cannot mean here that 'God' can be substituted for 'human being' in the above example as the cause of the existence of another human being. His reference to 'God' as the cause of the commencement and continuance of the existence of things must be taken in the sense of the 'ground' or 'origin' of existence, or "the first principle of nature" (*DIE* 75, 76). An explanation of the notion of 'ground' can perhaps be found by referring to *E* IV, 4, Dem. which suggests that God is the cause of the existence of man to the extent that the nature of man is a determinate expression of the nature of God, and it is not possible (logically) to conceive of a man existing without involving the nature of the principle of origin manifest in the effort by which he endeavors to preserve himself.

There are other statements of Spinoza's, in this connection, which clarify his position further. In *E* I, 28S, he observes that those things "which necessarily follow from His [God's] nature . . . must have been immediately produced by God." In the Appendix to *Ethics* (I) he says "That effect is the most perfect which is immediately produced by God, and in proportion as intermediate causes are necessary for the production of a thing is it imperfect." Now, since finite things cannot have followed from God's absolute nature, they must be the kind of things which are not immediately produced by God. Since he admits that God can be called a 'remote cause' of individual things "for the sake of distinguishing them from things which . . . follow from His absolute nature" (*E* I, 28S), he is implying that individual finite things cannot be said to have God as the cause of their existence in the same sense of 'proximate cause', as that in which one finite thing is said to be the cause of the existence of another.

Spinoza's statement about the notion of 'remote cause' is interesting in this context, even though he seems to be somewhat uncertain about its application. A 'remote cause', he says, is "that which is in no way joined to its effect" (*E* I, 28S). If this is the case, then it would follow that every use of the term 'cause', properly understood, must refer to an immediate or proximate cause and none other. Spinoza's distinction between things which "necessarily follow from the absolute nature of God," and those which do not so follow, would suggest that things of which God is the proximate cause are not and cannot be things which are finite.

In light of the above we must try to understand the statement "God is the immanent and not the transeunt cause of all things" (*E* I, 18). Clearly, when a finite thing is either produced by or is the cause of the existence of another finite thing, Spinoza would not deny that the relation involved is that of transeunt causation, as distinct from the immanent causation of God. The immanent causality of God, therefore, insofar as nothing can be nor be conceived without Him, must be taken in the sense of logically necessary conditions which provide the grounds for the relation of transeunt causality itself to hold between finite things.

The ambiguities in Spinoza's use of the term 'cause' sometimes create the impression that he maintained that since all things are logically determined by, and in that sense 'follow from', God, they therefore are also causally determined by God. This is a traditional misunderstanding of Spinoza which should be corrected. Although he does use the same word 'cause' in different contexts, no philosopher who uses it to refer to the kinds of distinctions which Spinoza makes would deny that the logical relation referred to by the use of the words 'determination' or 'follow from' is distinct in kind from the causal relation expressed by their use.

4.5

He admits that a finite modification of God is not identical with God *qua* infinite, and it is not God as an infinite reality that brings about or immediately causes the existence of a finite mode. Therefore when Spinoza says "God is the cause of all things," the word 'cause' in this statement must be understood in the sense of 'logical condition' (i.e., a condition that is conceptually necessary but which does not exist in the spatio-temporal sense of 'existence'), and not as the sufficient condition which immediately precedes, causes, produces or brings about, and, therefore, explains the existence of a finite mode in the common order of nature.

Spinoza does, indeed, say "God is the efficient cause of all things" (*E* I, 16 C1). Clearly, this cannot be taken to mean that he is claiming God to be the efficient cause of the existence of a human being in the sense that one human being is the efficient cause of the existence of another human being. These two senses must be kept distinct. For Spinoza, God is the efficient cause of the existence of a finite thing insofar as a finite thing is but a mode or a determinate manifestation of the nature of God, and hence without God can neither be nor be conceived; or insofar as all things that exist 'emanate' from God in the sense that God is their 'productive' condition, that is to say, their 'source' or 'origin'.

Spinoza takes the essence or nature of an individual thing to be a necessary condition of its existence, in the sense that once a thing has been brought about or produced by the causal action of other finite things, it is impossible for it not to exhibit the essential properties that characterize it as an individual of a certain definite kind. This essence or essential properties of the thing depend(s) in the last analysis upon the constitution of the primal reality of God; hence God is also considered to be the productive, emanative or efficient cause of the existence of finite things. Here again, God's efficient causality points to the 'source' or 'ground' for the operation of the relation of modal causation between finite things themselves, and is nothing other than 'logical determination' as distinct from 'causal determination', where the latter refers to the relation of dependence of one finite thing upon another.

4.6

It is appropriate now to examine the applicability of the above analysis of Spinoza's notion of cause to the issue of determinism with which it is closely related.

In discussing the problems of determinism and causal order, it is sometimes suggested that causes function as levers (of consciously self-directed behavior), where by "lever" means something that an agent may pull to change or control his environment to realize one practical possibility rather than another.[5] This is also the sense of the word 'cause' that Collingwood, for instance, suggests when he says "[T]hat which is caused is an event

[5]See, pp., A. Montefiore, "Determinism and Causal Order," *Proceedings of the Aristotelian Society* 58 (1957-58).

in nature; but the word 'cause' still expresses an idea relative to human conduct, because that which causes is something under human control, and this control serves as means whereby human beings can control that which is caused. In this sense the cause of an event in nature is the handle . . . by which human beings can manipulate it."[6]

Clearly, Spinoza's notion of 'cause' is wider than the sense of 'a lever which brings about an effect'. His view appears to be that a cause or reason is a logically necessary presupposition for the explanation of a thing that exists, or an action that takes place, even though it may not in fact be possible to point to, or empirically verify, a definite mode as its cause or reason in the sense of a 'lever'. The significant point to remember here is that since Spinoza accepts that man, as an agent, has the *power* and hence *is capable of bringing about certain effects* in the common order of nature, he would allow the term 'cause' to be used in the sense in which an agent has the ability, and in that sense *can bring about* certain changes in himself as well as in the world. "[E]very one has the power, partly at least, if not absolutely, of understanding clearly and distinctly himself and his affects and consequently bringing it to pass that he suffers less from them" (*E* V, 4S). That he does attribute this kind of power to man, enabling him to cause certain things to happen, is not to be denied. The difficulty arises when we try to reconcile the notion of logical determination of God with man's agency.

In the case of human behavior Spinoza's view is that the effects of a man's actions would not be what they are had he not acted as he did. He is not maintaining, of course, that no matter

---

[6]See Collingwood, R.G., *An Essay on Metaphysics* (Oxford, Clarendon Press, 1940), p. 296.

what a man did, the effect would be the same. He takes the cause or reason to be an indispensable condition of an effect. This does not imply, however, that a given effect cannot be produced by a variety of different conditions, or that a given set of conditions cannot explain a variety of effects. There is no evidence in Spinoza's writings to suggest that he would disagree that a human being as an agent can, and often does, act as a 'lever' to bring about certain changes in the world which would not have been brought about without his initiative.

It is, of course, possible to argue that in Spinoza's thought 'the pulling of the lever' is itself a part of the total situation, as determined as anything else by the nature of God. It needs to be noted, however, that the sense of 'determined' as it is used here involves a serious ambiguity. If 'determined' means that the pulling of the lever was *preordained* before the lever was actually pulled—implying that no matter what the agent's own inclinations, the pulling of the lever had to occur—then the use of that term is wholly unjustified and incompatible with Spinoza's views, for it disregards the distinction which Spinoza would wish to maintain between an 'event' and an 'action', as implied by the distinction he draws between adequate ideas and their relation to action (or activity), and inadequate ideas and their relation to suffering (or passivity) (*E* III, D2). If 'determined' is taken to mean that the pulling of the lever, as part of the total situation, must have some explanation in terms of causes or reasons as to why the pulling of the lever occurred as an event, or why the person pulled the lever, as an action, then there seems hardly any ground for objection; no one would reasonably want to hold that the pulling of the lever on the part of a person was an instance of an occurrence or action (a mode) whose existence could not be explained by reference to any set of conditions whatever.

Since Spinoza accepts the possibility of a human being

directing himself toward achieving a kind of perfection, in the sense of approximating the 'model' or 'ideal' he puts before his mind (*E* IV, Preface), he would agree that there is a sense in which for an individual to act to effect certain changes in himself and in the world is for him to *cause* himself and the world to be different from what it would be had he not acted as he did. It would be perfectly consistent with this to hold that, from another point of view, since every instance of mental and/or physical change must take place within the limits set by the nature of the universe as it is and the principle of its origin, it must be dependent upon, and in this sense 'determined by', the conditions which constitute the nature of the source and origin of the universe. This is the sense in which every mode must be considered as determined by God.

4.7

Plausible as this explanation may seem, there are some passages in the *Ethics* which would appear to be in serious conflict with it. The statement, for instance, that "Things could have been produced by God in no other manner than that in which they have been produced" (*E* , 33); or that "All things have been predetermined by God" (*E* I, Appendix), call for an explanation.

If we are to avoid being misled by them, these statements are best examined in their proper context. To clarify the meaning of the first of the above propositions, Spinoza explains "If . . . things could have been of another nature, or could have been determined in another manner to action, so that the order of nature would have been different, the nature of God might then be different to that which it now is, and hence that different nature would necessarily exist, and there might consequently be two or more God's, which is absurd" (*E* I, 33 Dem.). What Spinoza, evidently, means by this is that to conceive of the possibility of things being constituted differently than they in fact are, involves conceiving the possibility of another and differently constituted ultimate source, or origin, or God. The very idea of God being otherwise than He is conflicts with the self-sufficiency, completeness, or perfection of His nature. A God that could be otherwise than he is would not *be* God. He points out in the *Short Treatise* (I, 4), that to accept the possibility of God omitting to do anything, or doing something other than what he does, involves accepting that either he had a cause for it or that he did not. If he did have a cause for omitting to do it then it is necessary that he should omit doing it. If he has no cause to omit to do it then it is necessary that he should not omit to do it. "That is why," he says, "we deny *that God can omit to do what he does."* That is to say, it is not possible for God to do anything other than what he does. Spinoza is aware that "Some regard this as blasphemy, and as a belittling of God"; but he adds that "such an assertion results from a misapprehension of what constitutes *true freedom;* this is by no means what they think it is, namely, the ability to do or to omit to do something good or evil; but *true freedom is only, or no other than* [the status of being] *the first cause,* which is in no way constrained or coerced by anything else."

It follows, therefore, that reasons for actions performed by human beings and causes for occurrences and events in the universe are what they are because their very source or origin is constituted the way it is. In this sense everything is determined by the nature of the primary principle which is the explanatory condition of both *natura naturata* and *natura naturans.* Such a determination, it must be emphasized, has nothing whatever to do with the *power* or the *ability* of a human being to do otherwise than what he does. God's determination or causality, as we have seen, does not refer to the spatio-temporal relation of causality holding between finite modes.

4.8

Another point which Spinoza wishes to demonstrate is that "... [I]n things there is absolutely nothing by virtue of which they can be called cotingent" (*E* I, 33S). Now, before agreeing or disagreeing with him on this point, as on all others, we must be clear about exactly what he is asserting or denying. The history of the philosophical notions of 'contingent' and its correlative 'necessary' is filled with so much ambiguity and confusion that it is practically impossible to understand what a philosopher means by them without seeking further clarification.

What, we may ask, did Spinoza understand by 'contingent'? The definition that he gives of this notion is as follows: "I call individual things contingent insofar as we discover nothing, whilst we attend to their essence alone, which necessarily posits their existence or which necessarily excludes it" (*E* IV, D3). He also says that "... [a] thing can not be called contingent unless with reference to a deficiency in our knowledge" (*E* I, 33S).

Spinoza's concept of 'contingent' has been open to more than one interpretation. It is quite understandable to take his view to be that an individual thing, or a finite mode, is contingent in that we do not know whether its existence follows from its own nature, or whether its existence depends upon the existence of something else. So that when an individual thing is represented, or rather misrepresented, to our mind (or believed by us) to be one whose existence follows from its own nature, while, in fact, it is something which depends for its existence on something other than its own nature, then we are mistaken in our judgment about its character. To describe an individual thing as contingent is to commit precisely such an error; for in Nature, according to Spinoza, nothing is contingent, everything is necessary. This is a plausible view but I think an incorrect one.

Spinoza's concept of 'contingent' has to do, not with a thing being represented to our mind as uncaused, even though it is caused, but with *the essential character of an individual thing itself.* Man, for instance, is a finite mode, or an individual thing. When Spinoza says, "the essence of man does not involve necessary existence" (*E* II, A1), his reasons for saying this are that man, or any finite mode, can equally be conceived as existing or not existing. A thing which can be conceived as not existing cannot be the kind of thing that is self-dependent for its existence or *causa sui.* It is because the "essence of things produced by God does not involve existence" (*E* I, 24) (i.e., the existence of individual things does not follow from their own nature but depends on things other than themselves), and not that *we do not know* whether thier essence does or does not involve necessary existence, that an individual finite thing is to be called contingent. The "deficiency in our knowledge" of which Spinoza speaks in *E*I, 33S, in saying that ". . . a thing can not be called contingent unless with reference to a deficiency in our knowledge," does not refer to the state of any one's mind with respect to its causal conditions, but to the nature of the thing under consideration, namely a finite mode; hence every individual thing insofar as it depends for its existence upon causes external to its own nature, is necessarily contingent. Every action that a human being performs, in being a mode, is necessarily dependent for its existence upon reasons (causes) without which its existence could not be explained.

4.9

Spinoza's view of causation with respect to individual things must not be taken to imply that human beings cannot help doing what they do, which is, to use Nowell-Smith's expression, "one of the bogies that go under the name of determinism."[7] Spinoza does, indeed, hold that all things have necessarily flowed from God or " . . . [c]ontinually follow by the same necessity, in the same way as it follows from the nature of a triangle, from eternity to eternity, that its three angles are equal to two right angles" (*E* I, 17S). 'Predetermination' for Spinoza means 'eternally following from God'; this is the same as saying that it is logically necessary that the complete explanation of the nature and existence of each and every particular thing will involve reference to the first principle or the origin of the universe. Since such a conception of predetermination of all things by God does not have any relation to the thesis of fatalism, objections to Spinoza to this effect do not apply.

Confusion perhaps arises from thinking: "If it is logically necessary that the future should be what it is going to be, that is, it is logically impossible for it not to be what it is going to be, then there can be no point in doing anything, since whatever we do would have happened anyway, and whatever we do not do could not have occurred even if we had tried to make it happen." Clearly, this sort of thinking is a mistake, for although "whatever we are going to do must (logically) be going to happen—otherwise it could not be said that we are going to do it—it is seriously misleading to say that it must happen 'anyway', i.e., as if what is going to happen owes nothing to my efforts and activities."[8] What deprives man of the kind of freedom necessary for moral responsibility is the belief that no matter what a person does, he has neither any control over his own conscious behavior

---

[7]Cf. P.H. Nowell-Smigh, "Determinists and Libertarians," *Mind* 63 (1954) p. 331.

[8]Cf. R.D. Bradley, "Must the Future Be What It Is Going to Be?" *Mind* 68 (1959) p. 207.

nor can he do anything to alter the course of events. If, however, despite his belief that every event and action must have an explanation in terms of causes or reasons, Spinoza does allow that human beings have the ability or 'power' to make conscious efforts to bring about certain effects related to adequate and true ideas in thier minds (as I hope to show in the next chapter), then the crucial argument against him, namely,that his determinism implies a denial of moral freedom, becomes quite ineffective.

4.10

There is one other point in relation to the notion of 'contingency' which requires attention.

In the *Short Treatise* (I, 6), Spinoza's discussion of the nature of what he calls 'accidental things' is not only interesting but in some ways quite illuminating. His remark that "All things which are in Nature, are either things or actions" (*ST* I, 10), clearly suggests that Spinoza is not unaware of the distinction between things that are events and those that are actions. Spinoza seems to have a twofold division in mind about the nature of things in the world: (1) there are things that do take place; and (2) there are things that we imagine take place but which, in fact,do not. In regard to the first, we might say that although an event or an action did occur, we can imagine the circumstances and conditions under which it might not have taken place. There is certainly nothing odd or objectionable in speaking in this fashion. It does need to be understood, however, that when something does take place there is definitely a sequence of causes or reasons which can be referred to as an explanation and an answer to the question as to why it did in fact take place the way it did, depending on whether it is the causes or reasons that are relevant in response to the question. No one can reasonably maintain (barring miracles) that an action took place or an event occurred, but there is no possibility for there being any sequence of causes and reasons, the description of which would amount to answering the question of why it occurred.

In the case of the actions and events that do not take place, one might quite legitimately imagine circumstances under which they might have, and in that sense 'could have', taken place. In the case of an occurrence which can be *imagined* to have taken place, but in fact did not, no one can reasonably claim that there can be no possibility of an account being given as to why it did not in fact occur. The nonoccurrence of an action or event whose occurrence can easily be imagined by us must be accountable in terms of an answer to the question as to why it did not take place, by reference to the sequence of causes and reasons (or the absence of such causes and reasons) which would explain its nonoccurrence. No one, including Spinoza, would wish to deny that such acts of imagining things to have happened when they did not, and imagining things not to have happened when they did, are quite commonplace and people engage in them quite frequently.

In the *Short Treatise* (I, 6) Spinoza raises the question as to "whether there are in Nature any accidental things; that is to say, whether there are any things which," as he puts it, "may happen and may also not happen," and "whether there is anything concerning which we can not ask why it is." He answers by saying, "That which has no cause to exist cannot possibly exist; that which is accidental has no cause." He therefore concludes that in Nature there are no accidental things. By 'accidental things' he evidently means the kinds of contrafactual things that we can imagine to have happened but which in fact did not happen, and also the ones that we can imagine not to have happened but which in fact did happen. His point is that the sequence of causes and reasons required for the actual occurrence of things is manifestly absent in the case of things that we merely imagine occurring; hence they not only do not occur as we imagine them occurring, but unless the sequence of causes and reasons were itself different from what it in fact was, there is no way in which they could actually occur. In other words, his argument is that it is not the imagined different sequence of causes and reasons that brings about and explains an actual effect, but it is the actual sequence of causes and reasons that brings it about or explains it. To take things that are imagined to have happened as though they were things that actually happened is to confuse things which do not have the causal conditions to enable them to exist with things which do have causal conditions to enable them to exist. It is the imagined causal conditions that are related to accidental things. Since imagined causal conditions are not the ones that bring about the actual existence of things, Spinoza rightly concludes that accidental things do not exist in Nature. Or, as he puts it in other words, "In nature there is nothing contingent" (*E* I, 29).

4.11

There is hardly room to doubt that Spinoza makes a distinction between the kinds of necessity involved in the causal relation between finite things and God, and the causal relation between finite things themselves, even though he uses the same term, 'cause', to speak about these relations.[9] Thus the misrepresenta-

---

[9]See *Ep* 73 (and *E* I, 18) where Spinoza distinguishes the two senses of 'cause' by saying "I maintain that God is as they say the immanent cause of all things, but not the transeunt cause."

tion of Spinoza's thought occurs as a result of a failure to recognize that these two relations are not being claimed by Spinoza to be identical.

The difficulty in understanding his actual position with regard to the kind of determinism he professes to maintain seems to arise from statements of the kind where he appears to say that he sees no reason why human virtue cannot be acquired "as a result of fatilistic necessity, but only from the free decision of the mind" (*Ep* 58). Oldenburg, in one of his last letters to Spinoza expresses his concern on this point:

> You seem to assert the fatalistic necessity of all things, and actions; and they say that if this is admitted and affirmed then the nerves of all laws, of all virtue and religion are cut through and all rewards and punishment are empty. They think that whatever compels or involves necessity, also causes; and so they think no one would be inexcusable in the sight of God. For if we are driven by fate, and all things, turned by a strong hand, follow a definite and inevitable course then they can not see what place there is for blame or punishment. (*Ep* 74)

The way Spinoza begins his answer "I want to . . . explain in what sense I maintain the fatalistic necessity of all things and all actions" (*Ep* 75), suggests that the view Oldenburg attributes to Spinoza involves a misunderstanding which needs to be clarified. It also gives rise to a question about the kind of freedom Spinoza takes to be involved in freedom of the will, which his statements seeming to admit 'fatalistic necessity' appear to deny.

It becomes important, therefore, to take a closer look at Spinoza's concept of freedom and his views on the notion of freedom of will.

Chapter Five

Freedom

5.1

The sort of freedom involved in speaking of moral freedom is generally believed to consist of the feeling or awareness that human beings have of being able to choose betweeen alternative means to a desired end, or between alternative ends themselves, without consciousness of any psychological or physical compulsion.

In apparent disagreement with this common belief, Spinoza observes in the Appendix to *Ethics* I that "[M]an is born ignorant of the causes of things, and that he has a desire of which he is conscious, to seek that which is profitable to him. From this it follows, firstly, that he thinks himself free because he is conscious of his wishes and appetites, while at the same time he is ignorant of the causes by which he is led to wish and desire; and, secondly, it follows that man does everything for an end, namely, for that which is profitable to him, which is what he seeks" (see also *E* III, 2 S and *Ep* 58).

There is little doubt that Spinoza is maintaining that when we do not have adequate or true ideas of all the explanatory conditions of our behavior, that is to say, when our ideas of these conditions are inadequate and confused, we believe ourselves to have freedom of choice between alternatives. Spinoza is well aware that we (human beings) consider ourselves to be free, in this sense, at the level of common sense (or in his terms, at the level of imagination) rather than at the level of scientific or philosophical knowledge. In a letter written a few years before his death, he makes an interesting distinction between the common sense and philosophical levels. He observes:

> It is true that in the world we often act on conjecture; but it is false that our reflections are based on conjecture. In ordinary life we must follow what is most probable, but in philosophical speculation, the truth. Man would perish of thirst and hunger if he would not eat or drink until he had obtained a perfect proof that food and drink would do him good. But in contemplation this has no place. On the contrary, we must be cautious not to admit as true something which is merely probable. For when we admit one falsity, countless others follow. (*Ep* 56)

This is the distinction some modern philosophers suggest when they hold that what is true at the philosophical level need not be true at the level of common sense, and what is denied at the philosophical level, need not be taken as denied at the common sense level.[1] This is an important point to remember, because a

---

[1]Cf. P.H. Nowell Smith, "Determinists and Libertarians," *Mind*, 63 1954, pp. 318-321.

great deal of misunderstanding of Spinoza's views on moral freedom can be avoided if this distinction is kept in mind. Since contemporary philosophy is often associated with the notions of 'common sense' and 'ordinary language', there is an even greater risk of failing to understand Spinoza's views on this issue.

5.2

The examples that Spinoza offers in (*Ethics* III, 2 S) of the kind of conditions of our behavior which Spinoza says we are ignorant of when we believe ourselves to be 'acting freely', clearly suggest that the kind of 'causes' he is referring to are the explanatory conditions of our behavior that are other than our conscious desires and volitions. It cannot be denied that if we interpret human behavior in terms of such conditions alone then we cannot possibly distinguish between an 'event' and an 'action', and therefore cannot attribute moral value to human action any more than we can attribute it to the action of one billiard ball upon another. It is only when we regard the conscious desires of human beings as determining conditions or reasons, that is, factors which explain why men do what they do, that we can attach any moral value to their actions. In Chapter Three we showed that Spinoza accepts that human beings perform actions, that the notion of intentionality is applicable to some of their behavior, and thus men are not to be regarded merely as stones or trees.

It cannot be denied that when we are considering a man's behavior from a moral point of view, we must assume a certain degree of ignorance of those conditions which Spinoza refers to as 'causes'. By 'causes' he means causal conditions relating to the body, or physical causes. It must be accepted that the sphere of human behavior described as 'moral' is not that in which a man's behavior is regarded from the point of view of its physical causes.

If human actions are considered in terms of their physical con ditions alone, then they forfeit their claim to the application of moral epithets. Hampshire has rightly pointed out that "When the behavior now causally explained [in terms of physical causes] is what was formerly regarded morally wicked, we come to regard it as a symptom of a disease, curable, if at all, by the removal of its cause; expressions of moral disapproval come to seem useless and irrelevant."[2] When such actions were regarded with moral disapproval, those moral judgments were evidently based on ignorance of what Spinoza would call "causes other than conscious desires." It is indeed the case that the degree of man's responsibility and freedom diminishes with advancing knowledge of the causal conditions of his behavior other than his conscious desires. This does not imply, nor did Spinoza ever suggest, that one's desires are not to be regarded as reasons, and hence, as explanatory conditions of one's behavior. What is suggested is that one's conscious desires do not exhaust the conditions which explain an action as a finite determinate mode.

Although knowledge of ignorance of the causes of human behavior, other than conscious desires, does alter our moral judgments regarding a man's behavior, it does not follow that the mere assumption of such causes rules out the possibility or applicability of moral judgments altogether. Spinoza implicitly admits this in acknowledging that the necessity involved in assuming a complete explanation of every finite mode does not do away with either divine or human laws (see *Ep* 75). Moral precepts, he holds, are still salutary. That an action is fully explainable by reference to its conditions does not mean that evils which follow on wicked actions and feelings are less evil, that they will be

---

[2]S. Hampshire, *Spinoza* (Harmondsworth: Penguin 1951), p. 158.

feared less because they follow necessarily, or that we are not to judge such actions to be bad. The fact that we do make moral judgments is itself an expression of our nature as human beings derived from the primal reality or principle of origin of the universe. Spinoza is not saying it is senseless to maintain that any thing is good or bad, right or wrong; nor is he saying that all moral precepts are inadequate ideas, and that those who try to follow them are confused in their minds. It is highly misleading, if not false, to say that "Spinoza can allow no sense in which 'good' and 'bad' can be applied to persons which is not also a sense in which the words are applicable to any other natural object whether brutes or things. . . ."[3]

Spinoza does say that all individual things having a body are 'animate in different degrees' (*E* II, 13 S). Clearly, this does not mean (and the phrase 'in different degrees' is evidence for it) that all bodies have the same kind of ideas or mind. Inanimate objects cannot be said to be conscious in the sense in which animals are conscious. Although animals can be said to have consciousness, it is doubtful if they can be said to have *self*-consciousness. Of the animals that we know of so far, man alone is believed to be a *self*-conscious creature. By this it is meant that man not only can have ideas correlative to the affections of his body, but he can also have ideas of these ideas. He can be self-reflective, and modify his thought in the light of what he recognizes as criteria of certainty and truth. To imply that Spinoza believed 'good' and 'bad' must apply equally, and in the *same* sense, to man and every other creation or object in the universe, is to ignore the difference in kinds of modes, as well as differences of individuality in modes within a single category or attribute.

---

[3]Hampshire, *Spinoza*, p. 149.

Spinoza, it should be noted, speaks of "the true knowledge of good and evil insofar as it is true" (*E* IV, 14). By this he is to be taken to mean that a true knowledge of good and evil is a purely intellectual understanding of what is profitable, useful, or conducive to one's own interest and preservation. He also points out, in the demonstration to the same proposition, that it is not such knowledge considered merely as an idea in one's mind that can effect one's behavior. True knowledge of good and evil, he insists, can have a modifying effect on one's power of action *only insofar as it is considered as an affect.* We all claim, at various times, to know what is good and also what is right for us to do; yet we do something contrary to such knowledge, because the power of the affects or emotions by which we are led to act is greater than the power of our mere intellectual understanding. If, however, we were not merely intellectually certain of the truth of our ideas, but were also emotionally affected by this understanding, then it would be impossible for our desires to fail to conform to our knowledge. Then, we have not only a capacity or ability to do what we know we can in the light of our intellectual apprehension of good and evil, but we also have the desire and will to do it. As Spinoza puts it, "From the true knowledge of good and evil, *in so far as it is an affect* [and not in so far as it merely intellectually apprehended as true] necessarily arises desire, which is greater in proportion as the affect from which it springs is greater" (*E* IV, 15 Dem.). This desire, because it springs from our truly understanding something, follows in us, insofar as we act, and therefore must be understood by reference to our own nature as individuals having a mind.

Reason, or rationality for Spinoza, is the expression of a man's desire for self-assertion which follows from true ideas in his mind. We are self-determining and free to the extent that our conscious desires conform to these true ideas.

5.3

There are now two questions which require consideration. First, what exactly is Spinoza denying when he is said to have denied freedom of the will? Second, is his idea of human freedom compatible with the acceptance of moral distinctions that we normally make?

With regard to the first question it is initially important to take note of the following point. One of the main historical sources, if not the chief source, of misunderstanding of Spinoza's views on moral freedom seems to be that in the course of refuting Descartes' notion of freedom of the will[4] Spinoza maintained that the Cartesian notion of freedom implies a denial of causality. Spinoza's argument (as is clear from the contents of *Ep* 21 and 58) seems to be that Descartes, in holding that we are free to do this or that, or that we have freedom to choose between alternatives, admits to the fact of an uncaused mode in the form of an act of willing whose existence is in principle unexplainable. Spinoza's whole attempt, therefore, is concentrated upon showing the untenability of this stand by demonstrating that each and every particular thing as a finite mode must be caused to exist; that is, to be explainable by reference to some conditions which are independent of itself, for no particular thing can bring about its own existence and in that sense be self-explanatory. All finite modes, philosophically speaking, must include, in the explanation of

---

[4]Descartes' notion of freedom, Wolf rightly points out (in his commentary, *ST* p. 195), was the usual scholastic definition of freedom, namely, "*Cause libera potest agere quicquid, quantum, et quando lubet.* Heerboord (*Coll. Eth.*, P. 114, quoted by Sigwart) says distinctly that most philosophers defined free will as *facultas quae positis omnibus ad agendum requisitis potest agere et non agere, aut ita agere unum, ut contrarium agere posit.* Cf. Descartes, *Med.* IV."

their existence, reference to something other than themselves. Since Descartes' conception of freedom of the will involves positing a will that is uncaused, his view of the will as a mode free of its causal conditions must be mistaken.

It should be noted that in attacking Descartes' notion of freedom of the will, Spinoza not only fell short of refuting, but does not even seem to have intended to refute, or set aside, the concept of freedom of choice that is implied in moral contexts. Spinoza has, at best, argued against the view which involves the misunderstood freedom of the will, namely, the theory of the unexplainable, indifferent or irrational will. He has, therefore, through his argument, disproved or proved something quite different from what is required in order for his view to imply the rejection of moral freedom. To maintain, as he does, that apart from our conscious desires there are other factors—of which we are not aware or are ignorant—that are involved in the full explanation of our actions, does not imply, nor is it meant to be taken to imply, that conscious desires have no explanatory function in human actions, or that they are not to be regarded as 'causes' in any sense whatever. On the contrary, Spinoza, I think, would admit that evaluative terms can be appropriately applied only to behavior which requires reference to conscious desires in its explanation. Spinoza clearly admits in the preface to *E* IV that conscious desires can be considered as 'efficient causes' in the sense of 'reasons' which explain why we do what we do. Had Spinoza been inclined to reject the notion of 'freedom of choice' he could easily have maintained that in consciously choosing between different alternatives, we not only do not have a choice, but the consciousness of choosing, manifest in the exercise of our desires, is an illusion. This he does not try to do. What he does maintain is that the consciousness of freedom to choose is founded in that state of mind that is constituted of inadequate ideas, and therefore is not the same as that which he describes as "true freedom". This, however, means something entirely different.

He also wishes to maintain that even when our action is correlated with adequate ideas, we still retain the consciousness of our ability to choose. For him, this is not an illusion but a true idea of perception. There is no evidence to suggest that Spinoza intended to argue that when we are conscious of our ability to choose, we have a false perception of choice. What he does mean is that it is an inadequate idea, but not, for that reason, a false idea. Spinoza explicitly states that there is no error involved in the perceptions of the mind regarded by themselves. He gives the well-known example to clarify what he means by this:

> When we look at the sun, we imagine its distance from us to be about 200 feet, and in this we are deceived so long as we remain in ignorance of the true distance. When this is known, the error is removed, but not the imagination, that is to say, the idea of the sun which manifests its nature in so far only as the body is affected by it; so that although we know its true distance, we nevertheless imagine it close to us. . . . It is not because we are ignorant of the sun's true distance that we imagine it to be close to us but because the mind conceives the magnitude of the sun just in so far as the body is affected by it. . . . So *with the other imaginations by which the mind is deceived;* whether they indicate the natural constitution of the body or an increase or diminution in its power of action, *they are not opposed to the truth, not do they disappear with the presence of the truth.* (*E* IV, 1 S, my italics)

This explanation is also applicable to man's consciousness of freedom of choice. That is to say, insofar as man has the power or ability to form clear and distinct ideas—which all human beings have by virtue of the fact that there are some ideas which are necessarily adequate in each human mind (*E* V, 4 S) (namely the 'common notions' of which he speaks in the scholium to *E* II, 40, and which Spinoza rightly says "are the foundations of our reasoning")—it is correct to say that he can form (i.e., is *capable* of forming, or has the power to form) adequate ideas. Since the exercise of this power is already manifest in the fact of one's actually possessing some ideas that are adequate, the use of the term 'can' in the expression of this ability is clearly that of a nonconditional 'can'. Of course, man's success in forming more of such ideas does depend upon the requisite effort on his part. Spinoza's point seems to be that since the ability to make this effort is itself related to the active nature of the mind, expressed as desire or will logically related to adequate ideas, we are in the required sense 'free' to make the effort. It is a fact based upon the common observation that we are often 'free' in this sense, though not always so.

Furthermore, being hampered by our tendency to rationalize, we do not have the sort of freedom which Spinoza calls 'true freedom'. When men perceive themselves to be free in the sense that they are merely aware of their ability to choose one thing or another, but do not know what constitutes 'true freedom', then, so far as their imagination or perception is concerned, they are not being deceived nor are they committing an error. Even the man who is truly free, in Spinoza's sense of the word, would still retain the awareness of his ability to make (or not make) an effort consistent with his judgment of a given situation. This awareness is by no means an illusion, but an authentic idea of perception in the common order of nature. Given my immediate as well as inductive knowledge of myself and my thought processes, I may be perfectly certain that I shall do nothing contrary to what I know to be true. Yet it is in principle impossible to maintain that I cannot (in any sense of the term 'cannot') do anything other than what I actually do, should I want to do it. The fact that I would not want to do otherwise, does not rule out the intelligibility of the claim that if I wanted to, I could.

Spinoza's point is that when one acquires insight into the nature of true freedom—and he does not mean by this a mere intellectual understanding but an intellectual understanding together with the desire or the will corresponding to it—then, although one is indeed conscious of one's freedom to choose whether or not to do a certain thing, one will not do anything other than what follows from adequate ideas in one's mind. Just as the imagination or perception of the closeness of the sun persists even when one knows its true distance, the man who acts according to reason or adequate ideas is certainly conscious of his ability to do otherwise than what he does. However, since his will consists of desires logically related to adequate and true ideas, his actions are not a consequence of deliberating whether or not to do what he desires to do. His actions, in other words, do not follow from exercising his freedom to choose between alternatives, nor is he compelled by any external factors to do what he does. He acts by what Spinoza calls an 'internal necessity'.

Since to act according to reason is to be free from passive affects or passions, a man's actions which follow from adequate ideas are at once necessary and free. This is what Spinoza means when he says that 'necessary', in the sense of that which is in accordance with reason, and 'free', in the sense of that which follows from adequate ideas, are not contraries (*Ep* 56). "I do not place freedom," says Spinoza, "in free decision, but in free necessity" (*Ep* 58). In saying this, he is not by any means denying the reality of the consciousness of freedom of choice we commonly have. He is only emphasizing that at the level of 'adequate knowledge' the freedom of choice of which we are aware has no relevance whatsoever, for at that level we do not have to make a decision between doing and not doing a thing. In acting according to reason, he suggests, we must be free from the desire to do anything other than what is in accordance with reason. It is the kind of freedom in which choice is systematically limited to rational actions. This is what Spinoza means when he observes that it is of the nature of reason to consider things as necessary and not as contingent. (*E* II, 44 C 2).

It seems more than clear that in denying freedom of the will, Spinoza did not deny authenticity to a man's consciousness of freedom to choose between alternatives. He has denied will as a faculty different from and independent of the intellect. In fact, will, intellect, and mind would be regarded by him as abstractions. There exist only 'ideas', such as individual volitions, desires, thoughts, perceptions, imaginations, and so forth; these are what constitute mind. There is no relation between the consciousness of freedom of choice and what he calls 'true freedom' insofar as we can have all the freedom of choice in the world and yet not be truly free, in his sense of 'free'. The ability however, or the power to choose to be free in his sense of 'free', and hence to have the power to choose between the alternatives of freedom and bondage is the last thing that Spinoza wants to deny. If man did not have the ability to choose between these alternatives, Spinoza's sense of 'freedom' would have no meaning. Men are not born free, he tells us; they attain freedom (*E* V, 58 and S); the choice between making an effort to attain it or not is indeed theirs to make.

5.4

Man is naturally subject to passions; he follows the common order of nature, adjusting himself and his self-interests to the requirements of his environment (*E* IV, 4 C). The power of his passions is proportionate to the impact of the external world on his mind and body. He is subject to passions or passive emotions—insofar as these are created in him by objects outside himself—the nature of which he does not fully understand (*E* III,

1 Dem.). Passive emotion diminishes a man's power of rational response or action, whereas an emotion or affect which follows from an adequate understanding of the nature of objects increases one's power of action. Any action that follows from desire correlated with a passion, might also follow from a desire correlated with reason, and hence from an active emotion rather than a passive emotion (*E* IV, 59 and *E* V, 4 S). Since it is, in principle, impossible that our body be affected in any way for which an adequate explanation cannot be provided, and since every man has the power or ability, at least in part, if not absolutely, to have an adequate understanding of his own emotions, every man must be said to be capable of "bringing it to pass that he suffers less from them" (*E* V, 4 S).

The question now is how this control of passive emotions is to be brought about. Spinoza's answer is that we must make an effort to acquire as clear and distinct a knowledge of each emotion in ourselves as possible, so that our minds may grasp the conditions that brought it about. If our knowledge of the explanatory conditions of our emotions is adequate and true, then the affect of the mind correlative to this knowledge will necessarily give rise to a desire or will to act in a way which is consistent with our understanding. When we think truly, and our desires are correlated with true ideas of the nature of things, we shall necessarily be less agitated by our passions, shall have greater control over our responses to them, and therefore suffer less from them. Since to have adequate ideas or to understand truly includes (together with the intellectual grasp of the causes or explanatory conditions of our emotions and actions) the presence of desire or will corresponding to this understanding, it is in principle impossible that one have an adequate understanding of one's passive emotions and yet fail to act to be free of them. In this sense, to have adequate ideas means to be the adequate cause of one's actions. This is a logically necessary relation in Spinoza's concept of action.

5.5

To know things truly is to know their necessity, cause or explanation. Reason, by its nature, Spinoza tells us, considers things as necessary and not as contingent (*E* II, 44). It is not, however, clear what exactly he means by 'necessary'. There is perhaps a certain degree of ambiguity in his use of the term which requires consideration in discussing the issue of moral freedom.

Spinoza says, "A thing is said to be impossible either because the essence of the thing itself or its definition involves a contradiction, or because no external cause exists determinate to the production of such a thing" (*E* I, 33 S1). Accordingly, a thing is said to be 'necessary' when its existence follows "either from the essence and definition of the thing itself or from a given efficient cause." In a letter (*Ep* 12) Spinoza further points out that the existence of substance follows from its essence or definition, but the definition of modes cannot involve existence. Although modes or particular things exist, we can conceive them as nonexistent, hence, he says, "It is clear that we conceive the existence of substance as entirely different from the existence of modes." It seems, then, that since the existence of finite particular things does not follow from their essence or nature, they must, to that extent, be regarded as 'contingent'. Explaining the notion of 'contingent' Spinoza says, "I call individual things contingent insofar as we discover nothing while we attend to *their essence alone* which necessarily posits their existence or which necessarily excludes it" (*E* IV, D3, my italics). This clearly suggests that all finite modes must be regarded by him as 'contingent' in at least one sense of the term. They are contingent in the sense that their nonexistence does not involve contradiction. He would also insist that, insofar as finite things are 'necessary through their cause', they are at once contingent and necessary.

It seems that Spinoza does have in mind a distinction between two uses of the term 'necessary', and assumes such a distinction without making it clear in the same way as, for instance, Leibniz does. In his *Discourse on Metaphysics,* Leibniz distinguishes between that which is 'certain' and that which is 'necessary'.[5] He argues that everyone agrees that things which are going to happen in the future, that is, things which are contingent, must have a cause of their existence; but in admitting this, we do not admit that they are necessary. Necessity as involved in the essence of a thing, Leibniz tells us, is 'absolutely necessary', in that its opposite implies a contradiction. This is the sort of necessity that applies to mathematics and to eternal truths of geometry. The other, he says, "is only necessary *ex hypothesi,* but in itself is contingent, the contrary having not implication."

The distinction, as Leibniz points out, consists in the fact that the existence of a thing with a finite cause as its antecedent condition is 'assured' or 'certain,' but not 'necessary', since its opposite is not impossible in itself but impossible because of its cause. What happens, therefore, as an effect of a finite cause is not necessary in itself or through its essence; it was "[A]ssured that this would happen, but not that it is necessary in itself or that the contrary implies contradiction." A thing can be called 'necessary' only if its opposite is impossible because it is self-contradictory.

---

[5]Leibniz, *Discourse on Metaphysics,* trans. by P.G. Lucas and L. Grint (Manchester: Manchester University Press, 1953), Item XIII pp. 19–22. See also Leibniz's letter to Coste in 1707 on Necessity and Contingency, in *Leibniz,* Selections; ed. by Philip P. Wiener (New York: Scribners, 1951), pp. 480–485.

Spinoza acknowledges that we can conceive the nonexistence of this or that finite mode. He also states that from the fact that these modes now exist we cannot deduce whether they will or will not exist in the future, or that they existed or did not exist in the past (*Ep* 12). It seems that the distinction he had in mind between the two senses of 'necessary' was the same which Leibniz draws between what is 'necessary' and what is only 'certain'.

5.6

There is another distinction that Spinoza draws, in one of his letters between what he calls 'free necessity' and 'compelled necessity'. These correspond respectively to 'necessity' as applied to substance or God, and 'necessity' as applied to finite things. He further remarks in this letter: "[W]hen [someone] says with Descartes that he is Free who is compelled by no external cause, if by a man who is compelled he means one who acts against his will, I admit that in certain matters we are in no way compelled and *in this respect we have free will.* But if by compelled he means one who, although he does not act against his will, yet acts necessarily, then I deny that we are free in anything" (*Ep* 58, my italics). This is one of the most important of Spinoza's statements, since it is one place where Spinoza clearly admits to the application of the notion of 'free will' to men. We shall see whether the 'freedom' which he concedes in this passage is consistent with the concept of 'moral freedom' as it is ordinarily understood (where it is implied that 'one could have done otherwise').

According to the above passage, Spinoza would agree that when a man is not compelled by an external cause (for example, forced at the point of a gun) to do what he does, then so long as he does not act contrary to his wishes, he has free will.[6] When this man does what he consciously wants to do, however, and he therefore acts because he wishes or desires to do what he does, his action will also be 'necessary through a cause'. If this sense of 'necessary' is what is meant by 'compulsion', then we are always compelled. Spinoza's argument is that when a man acts according to his wishes and desires, and hence does what he wants to do without any external compulsion, he acts necessarily in the sense that his conscious desires are his reasons or sufficient conditions for doing what he does. Although it is true, in such a case, that he is not forced or coerced by an external cause, and to that extent has free will, he cannot be said to be free from the necessity of acting according to his wishes and desires. If a man decides not to do anything, then that in itself follows from his desires. No action, therefore, is free from the necessity of an explanatory condition. To the extent that our decision to act is not against our will, we do have free will. This does not mean, however, that our behaivor has no reason or 'cause', and is free in the sense of having no explanation.

From the above argument it should be clear that Spinoza does not deny that a man can be said to have free will when he does what he wishes to do, and when he is not forced or compelled by causes external to his body. What he means to emphasize by describing it as 'necessary'—, is that there must always be, in principle, some conditions which explain a man's action, and hence determine it. This, it should be noted, is not a radically

---

[6]Spinoza's use of 'compelled' here is not different from the ordinary use of 'compulsion'. Spinoza accepts the notion that a man is said to be compelled when he "[k]ills himself under compulsion by another when that other turns the right hand, with which the man had by chance laid hold of a sword, and compels him to direct the sword against his own heart" (*E* IV, 20S).

different position from that of a modern determinist, who finds the 'contra-causal' type of freedom incomprehensible.'[7] As Spinoza would agree, that to have discovered a reason or cause of an action in the form of one's desires is not necessarily to have discovered a compulsion but only an explanation, he would also agree that an action may have an explanation and yet be done out of free will.

5.7

In one of his letters to Spinoza, Tschirnhaus raises a question which seems pertinent to the issue of responsibility and punishment. Tschirnhaus insists that if men were always forced by external causes then no one would be able to acquire the habit of virtue. If this were granted, he adds, then all wickedness would be excusable (*Ep* 57).

Spinoza, in his reply (*Ep* 58), while firmly maintaining that unlike Descartes and Tschirnhaus, his own conception of human virtue is entirely consistent with the 'preordination of God', refers the reader, for elaboration of his views, to Part II, Chapter 8 of the *Appendix to The Principles of Descartes' Philosophy*.[8] The question to which Spinoza appears to address himself may be ex-

---

[7]See, for instance, R.E. Hobart, "Free Will as Involving Determinism," *Mind* 43 (1934) p. 1; P.H. Nowell Smith, "Free Will and Moral Resonsibility," *Mind* 57 (1948) p. 46; J. Wisdom, *Paradox and Discovery* Oxford: Basil Blackwell, 1965; Berkeley, Los Angeles, London: University of California Press, 1970), Ch. 2 on "Free Will".

[8]It is worth noting that as late as October 1674, when this letter was written, Spinoza was referring the correspondent to his *Cogitata* for an answer to a question. The reliance, therefore, which Spinoza shows on this early work of his indicates that, contrary to the generally held opinion, the *Cogitata* is not to be regarded as unreliable for Spinoza's views on certain points.

pressed in the following way: If human beings act out of necessity in the sense that their actions follow from their nature which they derive from God, and evil acts must also be said to follow from the same nature that we derive from divine law, then why is it that wicked people are punished? In other words, why are human beings held responsible for evil actions when they do what they do in accordance with divine law and hence could not have acted otherwise?

The answer to this question, Spinoza suggests, is that men are also punished according to the divine law. This answer is much too brief and baffling. What he appears to be saying, however, becomes clearer when we consider his additional remark to the effect that, if someone holds that only those should be punsihed whom we believe to have committed wrong through their own will alone, then "Tell me," Spinoza asks, "why do men try to exterminate poisonous snakes who offend only through their nature and could not do otherwise?" What he seems to mean is that human beings punish and hold one another responsible for their actions because, in thc final analysis, it is part of their very nature to punish for behavior which they believe to be wicked. Thus, whatever men do, they do it by the 'laws' which are the explanatory principles of the universe. Since human behavior must ultimately be explainable by reference to the principle of the origin of the universe, the effects follow from it necessarily. There is at least one sense of the question, therefore, in which to ask "why do men punish?" is of no practical significance. Punishment is inflicted on the wicked because human beings, constituted as they are, cannot help punishing people whom they believe to be wicked. This sort of metaphysical explanation is precisely what may be described by some as Spinoza's "doctrine of absolute determinism," a phrase which seems to have an emotional overtone that tends to generate a contra attitude towards the view. It is used often as a term of ridicule or rejection on grounds which are seldom, if ever, philosophical. It seems to me that absolute determinism as a philosophical doctrine can only be maintained at the expense of the distinction between two kinds of 'necessity' discussed earlier, a distinction with which Spinoza was well acquainted, as we have seen.

It will be recalled that individual things, of whatever kind, are held by Spinoza to be contingent by their very nature, essence, or definition. At the level of reference to human actions as finite modes falling into the category of 'contingent' things, Spinoza must, and does, allow that, granting the ability and the will, a human being has reasons for doing what he does, can choose to do what he wishes or desires, and therefore has free will insofar as he is not forced by something external to himself. In light of the explicit statements referred to in Spinoza's letter to Tschirnhaus, where he states that a man has free will to the extent that he does what he desires to do and is not compelled by any external force, any argument to the effect that Spinoza does not or cannot allow this sort of freedom would appear to involve a profound misapprehension of his thought.

5.8

Spinoza makes another attempt to reconcile his notion of 'necessity' with the concept of action involving free will. In another one of his letters he observes that the

> [I]nevitable necessity of things sets aside neither divine nor human laws. For moral precepts, whether they receive the form of law from God himself, or not, are nevertheless divine, and salutary; and whether we receive good[. . .]from the necessity of divine nature, it will not therefore be either more or less desirable, just as, on the other hand, the evils which follow

> from evil deeds are not to be feared any the less because they follow from them necessarily. (*Ep* 43)

He makes the same point, almost word for word, in one of the last letters he wrote to Oldenburg in December 1675 (*Ep* 75). Here again he adds that "whether we do what we do necessarily or contingently, we are nevertheless led by hope and fear."

In saying that moral laws are divine, Spinoza is not to be taken to mean that moral precepts of the kind one finds, for example, in the Ten Commandments, were given to human beings by God in the way that legislature or kings give laws to the people. Such an analogy (as we saw in Chapter One) is entirely misleading. What he must be taken to mean is that since 'appetite', *conatus* or impulse to self-preservation is the very foundation of all man-made rules or laws, and since *conatus* is the essence of man following from the principle of origin of the universe as a whole, the laws which human beings devise for themselves in following their *conatus* are, in their ultimate analysis, 'divine' laws. A moral rule, principle or precept is 'divine' in the derivative sense, as it serves men's interests which they preserve by virtue of their very nature. A moral law, as derivatively divine, is to be distinguished from a divine law in the primary sense in that, while the former is formulated and devised by human beings in their own interests, the latter does not exist for the sake of any end or interest. A divine law is divine precisely in the sense that it is identical with the eternal nature of the primal reality or God. God does not act for the sake of an end, for God is not the kind of reality about which it makes any sense to say it can have an interest in an end or purpose. Human laws are indeed formulated with an end in view, namely to be conducive to man's preservation. Therefore, while it makes sense to say that one ought to obey the law devised by human beings in a particular society (which is a 'prescriptive' law), it does not make sense to say that one ought to obey the divine law. Divine law is obeyed or observed necessarily, not in the sense that one is compelled by external forces to abide by it, but in that all things exist and act in accordance with it necessarily, though without compulsion. It is also in this sense that Spinoza observes "*necessary* and *free* are not contraries" (*Ep* 56 and 21). Necessity, for him, is not opposed to, but compatible with freedom, while freedom and coercion (or compulsion) are taken by him to be incompatible.[9]

When it is said of a human being that a certain action of his was 'avoidable' or that he 'could have done otherwise', it is not being denied that there must be some explanatory conditions by reference to which the action, as an effect that actually occurred, can be understood. There is nothing whatsoever in the notion of 'cause' itself which involves constraint or compulsion, even though it may involve a kind of necessity. As it is clear from Spinoza's conception of 'accidental things' discussed toward the end of the last chapter, and as C.L. Stevenson rightly points out,[10] avoidability in this context is concerned with what would have happened if a choice that was not made had been made. Since the 'if' clause is manifestly contrary to fact, it does not deny that the actual choice may have been determined by preceding events. The question to be considered now is whether, and in what sense Spinoza would consider it meaningful to say that a man could have done otherwise than he did or could have made a choice

---

[9]It is interesting to compare David Hume on this point. Hume observes that liberty as opposed to constraint must be distinguished from liberty as opposed to necessity; and man, says Hume, has liberty when he is not constrained. See *Enquiry Concerning Human Understanding,* Ch. VIII end of Pt. I.

[10]See C.L. Stevenson, *Ethics and Language* (New Haven: Yale University Press, 1944), Ch. XIV.

other than the one he made. Granting that had he made a different choice, he would have acted differently, can we then hold a man responsible, and therefore blameworthy, for not having made such a choice?

To answer these questions we need to remember that Spinoza clearly states (in *E* V, 4 S) that all human beings are capable, in whatever limited way, of thinking clearly and distinctly. Insofar as this is the case, a man who has acted on a desire related to inadequate and false ideas must certainly be considered capable of acting on a desire related to adequate and true ideas. The sense of 'could have done otherwise' involved here cannot be denied; nor does the ability to have adequate and true ideas require testing or verification in order for us to assert that he has it. Therefore, if our observation, together with a man's own account of his behavior, shows that he had faulty understanding of the relevant factors in the situation, we can properly say that he could have had true understanding.

It should be noted, however, that the ability or power to entertain true ideas is one thing, while thc ability to desire or will to act in accordance with true ideas, is quite another. We all rightly claim at various times that we know what we should do in order for our actions to be consistent with our knowledge, yet we fail to do it. This knowledge is no more than a purely intellectual understanding, and it does not need to be verified and tested for our claim to such knowledge to be true. Under these circumstances there is a sense in which it is possible to say that although we do not, in fact, have the desire or the will to conform with our understanding, we *could* have such a desire. This latter claim, however, unlike the claim to knowledge, is scarcely intelligible in the absence of a test. The only test of whether we could have the desire consistent with the knowledge or understanding we claim to have, is whether or not we actually act in accordance with it. I may rightly claim to know, for instance, that smoking is bad for my health. I know that I know this. I do not need to produce any evidence whatsoever for my claim to know this to be true. No tests or verifications are necessary for authenticating such claims to knowledge. I may also wish to give up the habit and give expression to my wish by saying "I want to quit smoking." Yet, I may lack the will or desire to do it. I may claim that I could do it, meaning, I could have the will to do it, but the only way in which this can be taken to be a genuine claim is when I do, in fact, stop smoking.

Now 'desiring' and 'willing' are regarded by Spinoza to be identical, and are to be distinguished from mere 'wishing'. To say "I could have done otherwise," when this gives expression to the mere wish to have done otherwise than I did, is perfectly legitimate. The claim "I could have done otherwise," where it amounts to an expression of a wish (as distinct from the desire or will), does not require authentication by any test anymore than my claim to knowing (that smoking is bad for my health) needs to be tested in order for it to be true. It is not the 'wishing' that is related to action, but 'desiring' or 'willing'. Spinoza's contention is that it is not mere knowledge or true ideas, anymore than wishes, that bring about an action, but it is the desire that conforms to my knowledge that does so. Insofar as a man is granted the ability to have true ideas, it is correct to say that he could improve his understanding; the desires correlated to such understanding, and actions related to those desires would then be different. In this *Treatise on the Improvement of the Understanding,* Spinoza clearly assumes the applicability of this sense of 'could' where it relates to the possibility for men to have true ideas. He also maintains that desires cannot be altered without an alteration in the understanding itself; hence, acitons, which necessarily follow from desires, cannot be otherwise than what they are in the absence of modification in the understanding.

5.10

The point made above is closely related to a consideration of the second question that was raised, namely, whether Spinoza's concept of human action allows for the kind of moral distinctions we ordinarily make in terms of the notions of responsibility and blame.

Let us take, for example, a man who is held responsible for having done something that he desired to do. The reasons for holding him responsible include the assumption that there was no external physical compulsion involved and the person acted "of his own free will." Since he was not forced to do what he did, we say that, had he wanted or desired to refrain from doing what he did, he could have acted otherwise. Thus, wherever it applies that a man could have done otherwise, we can also say that he is responsible for doing what he did.

Since an action a person performs is related to his desires (in the sense that the action must be what he desires to do), and desires are necessarily related to one's knowledge or understanding (constituted of ideas in one's mind that are adequate and/or true and inadequate and/or false), then to maintain that a person can *act* otherwise than he does, when the desires that relate to his action are a necessary consequent of the knowledge that constitutes his mind, is to misconstrue seriously the situation. Unless an emendation in the ideas that constitute his mind is brought about, the possibility of the desires being different from what they are is necessarily ruled out. If the desires in themselves cannot be different in light of the ideas that constitute a person's mind, then to say that a person could act otherwise is to give a highly misleading, if not false account of the matter.

The question therefore must be asked as to what it is we are referring to when we say that a person *could have done* otherwise. Spinoza's answer appears to be that we cannot be referring to the *action* a person performs. The action is related to the desires, and the desires being what they are, it is in principle impossible for the action to follow from the desires that a person does not in fact have.

In referring to a person's ability to have different desires, to suggest that he could desire differently, indicates a failure to grasp the necessary relation between desire or will and knowledge or ideas in his mind. In other words, the desires themselves cannot be altered without altering the understanding or the system of ideas in the mind.

If we maintain that what we are actually referring to when we say that a person "could have done otherwise" is the person's ability to have true ideas when he has false ones, then we are saying, in effect, that he could have had true ideas or that it was within his power to acquire true knowledge. This is admittedly correct to a partial extent, and Spinoza himself agrees to it (see *E* V, 4 S), but since it is possible, as we have seen, to have a true idea or knowledge and still not have the desire consistent with it, then merely having a true idea does not by itself, result in a corresponding desire to act (*E* IV, 14 Dem.). Since the only sense in which the judgment "he could have done otherwise" is truly applicable, with regard to a person's desire or will, when it is *testable* by a person's actually doing what we think he has the ability to desire to do, the judgment that he could have willed to do otherwise, in the absense of such a test, seems quite misplaced.

If our attribution of responsibility or blame is based upon the claim that in any instance of action which men perform of their own free will and without external compulsion, the judgment that they could have done otherwise is also applicable, then our conception of free action itself, Spinoza suggests, is seriously mistaken. Whether our action is free does not depend on the applicability of whether we could have done otherwise. It is not meaningful to speak of the ability to 'act otherwise' in terms that are independent of 1) desire, in the absence of which an action cannot take place, and 2) the system of ideas constituting a mind that explains the desire.

We have observed that Spinoza maintains that all men are partially capable of having true knowledge or true ideas, and of having desires that conform with them. There is a sense, therefore, in which it is within the power of any man to 'act upon reason'. But if we merely say of a person that he could act on reason, without stating or indicating the method by which he can do so, the 'could' judgment is incomplete and involves an inadequate understanding of human behavior. Spinoza, therefore, seems to suggest that to say a man could have acted otherwise implies a demand for an answer to the question "by what method could he be led to modify the desires and therefore act otherwise than he did?" Unless one has stated the method of modification of desires, the claim that a man could have done otherwise is vacuous; in the absence of a provision of such a method, the judgment about his ability to act otherwise remains unintelligible.

Spinoza shows that there is a method by which men can bring about a modification in their desires and actions. The details of the method are laid down in the first ten propositions of *Ethics*, Part V. We shall not be concerned here with an examination of the method, which requires a whole book in itself, but with the general implications of this method insofar as it pertains to the issue of moral freedom.

To the extent that what we do can be explained by reference to our desires, and we are not compelled by any external agent, we are responsible for our action. The action follows from our desires. These are related to our knowledge of the nature of things in the world, which includes knowledge of ourselves and our situation, however adequate or inadequate. Spinoza's point is that to have 'freedom' to do what one wants is to have freedom in a very limited sense. 'True freedom' consists of the cultivation of desires that are related to true ideas in one's mind insofar as the knowledge constituting such ideas is not merely an intellectual understanding, but an active emotion or an effect as well. We attain true freedom to the extent that our actions can be understood by reference to our desires that are related to adequate and true ideas in our minds, and of which, therefore, we ourselves, as constituting a union of mind and body, are the adequate cause.

It is in light of this method of modification of desires, and hence of actions in accordance with one's power of reason, that 'could' judgments are relevant in the only significant sense—one which cannot be applied to them in the absence of a clear method of such modification and improvement. The only way to discover whether a man is capable of making use of the method, and thus, whether the judgment "he could have done otherwise" is applicable to him, is not merely through insisting that he *could* have, or by claiming that his action was done of his own free will. One must find whether a man has not only the capacity but also the will to have true knowledge of himself and his affects, as well as the will to act on it. Spinoza's description of the character of a 'truly free' individual (*E* IV, 67–73) is meant, among other things, to assist us in discovering whether a man does or does not act in accordance with reason.

5.11

It remains to note that an individual who is free, in Spinoza's sense of 'free', is still a step below the highest kind of freedom. An action in accordance with reason follows from the desire correlative with a knowledge of the necessity of the existence of things through their causes. When, however, we understand the existence of particular things, not by reference to the necessity of their causal conditions, but by reference to their own essence or nature, then our understanding or knowledge is identical with knowledge in the 'infinite intellect of God'. This kind of knowledge or, more accurately, insight, does not proceed from knowledge of the causes or explanatory conditions of particular things; rather it arises through understanding the nature of the categories under which we experience particular things in the world. Such knowledge, as Spinoza puts it, "advances from an adequate idea of the . . . essence of certain attributes of God to the adequate knowledge of the essence of things" (*E* II, 40 S2). To know the existence of things as following from their essence is to know things as they are in themselves. For Spinoza, one "who knows things by this kind of knowledge passes to the highest human perfection and consequently is affected with the highest joy" (*E* V, 27 Dem.). At the stage of knowledge where every particular thing is understood to exist as a consequence of its very nature or essence, it becomes as absurd to blame an individual for any of his actions as it is to condemn a triangle for not having the properties of a circle.

This part of Spinoza's philosophy has always been susceptible to misinterpretation. Spinoza does not mean to say that no human being, as a matter of fact, ever has or should have a right to blame or praise anyone; or that nothing should ever be considered good or bad, or that no one can or should be held responsible for his actions. He is maintaining that if one understood why a thing is what it is, by reference to an insight into the nature or constitution of the thing itself, one would also understand why it is necessary that it must be what it is. An earthquake, a flood, a cancer, a nuclear bomb, a war, understood in this way, are not, in themselves, evil. They are considered evil because they have a certain painful effects on us and other creatures.

Now Spinoza does not mean that an individual human

being, who has not attained this level of understanding and the accompanying attitude of mind, would or should regard nothing as good or evil, right or wrong. At the level of understanding from which we regard things as just and unjust, praiseworthy or blameworthy (the level of partly inadequate or confused, and partly adequate knowledge), Spinoza would certainly admit that notions such as 'freedom of choice', 'responsibility', 'punishment', 'avoidability', 'sin', 'merit', and so on, are important and useful (*E* IV, 37 S2). In order "that men may be able to live in harmony and be able to help one another, it is necessary for them . . . to beget confidence one in the other that they will do nothing by which one can injure the other" (*E* IV, 37 S2). Since man, being part of Nature, is subject to desires and other affects and changes by reference to things external to himself (*E* IV, 4 C), and reason or true knowledge by itself cannot restrain an affect or a desire, but one affect or desire alone can restrain another (*E* IV, 14 Dem.), it is necessary for harmonious existence that human beings be restrained from desiring to do injury to themselves or to others through (the affect of) fear of greater injury to themselves in the form of punishment or penalty (*E* IV, 37, S2). Within the context, therefore, of laws formulated by human beings to govern their lives more peacefully, "it is necessary to consider things as contingent" (*TPT*, Ch. 5); human beings must be said to have freedom to do or not to do things in obedience to such laws, according to their wishes. If this is what is meant by 'freedom of the will', then Spinoza neither meant to deny, nor would it be philosophically consistent for him to deny it. He would add, however, that such freedom will never give us the peace of mind and blessedness which accompany freedom from passions, since that comes only from having one's desires and will conform to true knowledge.

Since the power to attain true knowledge is partially granted to all human beings, we are ourselves responsible for the failure to exercise this power, and hence have no one but ourselves to blame for remaining in slavery rather than living in freedom.

Selected Bibliography

Works on Spinoza

Original Latin

Opera. Ed. by J. Van Vloten and J.P.N. Land. 4 vols. The Hague, 1914.

Opera. Ed. by Carl Gebhardt. 4 vols. Heidelberg, 1925.

English Translations

The Chief Works of Spinoza. Trans. by R.H. Elwes. London, 1906.

Correspondence of Spinoza. Trans. by A. Wolf. London, 1928

Ethics. Trans. by A. Boyle. London, 1910.

Ethics. Trans. by W.H. White and A.H. Sterling. Oxford, 1927.

The Political Works of Spinoza. Trans. by A.G. Wernham. Oxford, 1958.

The Principles of Descartes' Philosophy and *Colgitata Metaphysica.* Trans. by H.H. Briton. Chicago, 1905.

Short Treatise on God, Man and His Well-Being. Trans. by A. Wolf. London, 1910.

Books

Alexander, Samuel. *Spinoza and Time.* London, 1921.

Spinoza; An address. Manchester, 1933.

Allison, Henry E. *Benedict De Spinoza.* Boston, 1975.

Bidney, David, *The Psychology and Ethics of Spinoza.* New Haven, Connecticut 1940.

Bourget, Paul. *Spinoza.* Chicago 1912.

Browne, Lewis. *Blessed Spinoza.* New York, 1932.

Caird, J. *Spinoza.* Edinburgh, 1910.

Curley, E.M. *Spinoza's Metaphysics.* Cambridge, Massachusetts 1969.

DeDeugd, C. *The Significance of Spinoza's First Kind of Knowledge.* Netherlands, 1966.

Duff, Robert. *Spinoza's Political and Ethical Philosophy.* Glasgow, 1903.

Feuer, Lewis Samuel. *Spinoza and the Rise of Liberalism.* Boston, 1958.

Friedlander, M.H. *Spinoza, His Life and Philosophy.* London, 1887.

Gueroult, Martial. *Spinoza, Tome I: Dieu (Ethique I).* Paris, 1968.

______. *Tome II: L'Ame.* Paris, 1974.

Gunn, J.A. *Benedict Spinoza.* New York, 1925.

Hallett, H.F. *Aeternitas, A Spinozistic Study.* Oxford, 1930.

———. *Benedict de Spinoza. The Elements of His Philosophy.* London, 1957.

———. *Creation, Emanation and Salvation, A Spinozistic Study.* The Hague, 1962.

Hampshire, Stuart. *Spinoza.* Harmondsworth, 1951.

Harris, E. *Spinoza, Salvation from Despair.* The Hague, 1973.

Hubbeling, H.G. *Spinoza's Methodology.* Netherlands, 1964.

Joachim, H.H. *A Study of the Ethics of Spinoza.* Oxford, 1901.

———. *Spinoza's Tractatus de Intellectus Emendatione.* Oxford, 1940.

Kayser, Rudolf. *Spinoza.* New York, 1968.

Kline, George. *Spinoza in Soviet Philosophy.* London, 1952.

Knight, W. *Spinoza.* London, 1882.

Levin, Dan. *Spinoza.* New York, 1970.

Martineau, J. *A Study of Spinoza.* London, 1882.

McKeon, Richard. *The Philosophy of Spinoza.* New York, 1928.

McShea, Robert J. *The Political Philisophy of Spinoza.* New York, 1968.

Melamed, S.M. *Spinoza and Buddha.* Chicago, 1937.

Meyers, H.A. *The Spinoza-Hegel Paradox.* Ithaca: New York, 1944.

Oko, Adolph. *The Spinoza Bibliography.* Boston, Massachusetts, 1964.

Parkinson, G.H.R. *Spinoza's Theory of Knowledge.* Oxford, 1954.

Picton, J.A. *Spinoza; A Handbook to the Ethics.* London, 1907.

Pollock, F. *Spinoza, His Life and Philisophy.* London, 1880.

———. *Spinoza.* London, 1935.

Powell, E.E. *Spinoza and Religion.* Chicago, 1906.

Roth, Leon. *Spinoza, Descartes and Maimonides.* Oxford, 1924.

______. *Spinoza.* London, 1929.

Runes, D.D. *Spinoza: Dictionary.* New York, 1951.

Saw, Ruth L. *The Vindication of Metaphysics; A Study in the Philosophy of Spinoza.* London, 1951.

Shanks, Alexander. *An Introduction to Spinoza's Ethics.* London, 1938.

Strauss, Leo. *Spinoza's Critique of Religion.* Berlin, 1930; New York, 1965.

Sullivan, Celestine J., Jr. *Critical and Historical Reflections on Spinoza's "Ethics".* Berkeley, 1958.

Wetlesen, J. *A Spinoza Bibliography.* Oslo, 1971.

______. *The Sage and the Way.* Assen, Netherlands, 1979.

Wolf, A. ed. and trans. *The Oldest Biography of Spinoza.* London, 1927.

Wolfson, Abraham. *Spinoza, A Life of Reason.* New York, 1932.

Wolfson, H.A. *The Philosophy of Spinoza.* Cambridge, Massachusetts 1934.

Anthologies of Essays and Articles on Spinoza

Bend, J.G. van der, ed. *Spinoza on Knowing, Being and Freedom.* Proceedings of the Spinoza symposium at the International School of Philosophy in the Netherlands, Leiden, September 1973. Assen: Netherlands: 1974.

Grene, M., ed. *Spinoza: A Collection of Critical Essays.* New York, 1973.

Hessing, S. *Speculum Spinozanum.* London, 1977.

Inquiry XII (1969). Oslo, Universitetsforlaget.

Inquiry XX (1977) Oslo, Universitetsforlaget.

Kashap, S.P., ed. *Studies in Spinoza, Critical and Interpretive Essays.* Berkeley, 1972.

Kennington, R., ed. *The Philosophy of Baruch Spinoza.* Washington, D.C. 1980.

Freeman, E. and Mendelbaum, M., eds. *Spinoza: Essays in Interpretation.* Illinois, 1973.

Philosophia 7, March 1977: 1–161.

Shahan, R. and Biro, J., eds. *Spinoza, New Perspectives.* Oklahoma, 1978.

Wetlesen, J., ed. *Spinoza's Philosophy of Man.* Assen, Netherlands, 1978.

Wilber, J.B. *Spinoza's Metaphysics: Essays in Critical Appreciation.* Assen, Netherlands, 1976.

Other Articles and Reviews

Balz, A.G. "Cartesian Refutations of Spinoza." *Philosophical Review* 46 (1937): 461–484.

Bidney, David. "Value and Reality in the Metaphysics of Spinoza." *Philosophical Review* 45 (1936): 229–244.

______. "Joachim on Spinoza's Tractatus de Intellectus Emendatione." *Philosophical Review* 51 (1942): 47–65.

Broad, C.D. "Hallett's Aeternitas." [two articles] *MIND* 42 (1933): I: 150-169; II: 299–318.

Copleston, F.C. "Pantheism in Spinoza and the German Idealists." *Philosophy* 21 (1946): 42–56.

deBurgh, W.G. "Great Thinkers. VIII: Spinoza." *Philosophy.* II (1936): 271–288.

Eisenberg, Paul D. "How to Understand De Intellectus Emendatione." *J. of History of Philosophy* 9 (1971): 171–191.

Feibleman, James K. "Was Spinoza a Nominalist?" *Philosophical Review* 60 (1951): 386–389.

Floistad, G. "The Knower and the Known." *Man & World* 3 (1970) 3–25.

Hallett, H.F. "Spinoza's Conception of Eternity." MIND 37 (1928): 283–303.

______. "Knowledge, Reality and Objectivity: II." MIND (1940): 303–332.

______. Review of Bidney's *The Psychology and Ethics of Spinoza. MIND* 50 (1941): 385–393.

______. "Some Recent Criticisms of Spinoza." [three articles] *MIND* 51 (1942): I: 134–159; II: 223–243; III: 319–342.

______. "Some Recent Criticisms of Spinoza." *MIND* 52 (1943): 1–23.

Hicks, G. Dawes. "The 'Modes' of Spinoza and the 'Monads' of Leibniz." *Proceedings of the Aristotelian Society* 18 (1917-18): 329–362.

Hampshire, S.N. "A Kind of Materialism." Presidential address in Proceedings and Addresses of A.P.A. 63 (Sept. 1970) 5–23.

Jonas, Hans. "Spinoza and the Theory of Organism." J. *of History of Philosophy* 3 (1965): 43–57.

Kaufmann, Fritz. "Spinoza's System as Theory of Expression." *Philosophy and Phenomenological Research* 1 (1940-41): 83–97.

Latta, R. "On the Relations between the Philosophy of Spinoza and that of Leibniz." *MIND* 8 (1899): 333–356.

MacIntyre, A. "Spinoza." In *Encyclopedia of Philosophy* Paul Edwards (ed.), vol. 7. New York, 1967: 530–541.

Mackinnon, Flora Isabel. "The Treatment of Universals in Spinoza's Ethics." *Philosophical Review* 33 (1924): 345–359.

McKeon, Richard. "Causation and the Geometric Method in the

Philosophy of Spinoza." [Two articles] *Philosophical Review* 39 (1930): I: 178–189; II: 275–296.

McShea, Robert J. "Spinoza on Power." *Inquiry* 12 (1969): 133–143.

Modak, M.S. "Spinozistic Substance and Upanishadic Self." *Philosophy* 6 (1931): 446–458.

Murray, J. Clark. "The Idealism of Spinoza." *Philosophical Review* 5 (1896): 473–488.

Naess, Arne. "Freedom, Emotion and Self-Subsistence: The Structure of a Small, Central Part of Spinoza's Ethics." *Inquiry* 12 (1969): 68–104.

Natanson, Harvey B. "Spinoza's God: Some Special Aspects." *Man & World* 3 (1970): 200–223.

Parkinson, G.H.R. "Language and Knowledge in Spinoza." *Inquiry* (1969): 15–40.

Pearson, Carl. "Maimonides and Spinoza." *MIND* 8 (1883): 338–353.

Pollock, Frederick. "Notes on the Philosophy of Spinoza." *MIND* 10 (1878): 195–212.

Radner, Daisie. "Spinoza's Theory of Ideas." *Philosophical Review* 80 (1971): 338–359.

Ratner, Joseph. "Spinoza on God." [Two articles] *Philosophical Review* 39 (1930): I: 56–72; II: 153–177.

Rice, Lee C. "The Continuity of 'Mens' in Spinoza." *The New Scholasticism* 43 (1969): 75–103.

Ritchie, Eliza. "Notes on Spinoza's Conception of God." *Philosophical Review* 11 (1902): 1–15.

______. "The Reality of the Finite in Spinoza's System." *Philosophical Review* 13 (1904): 16–29.

Roth, Leon. "Spinoza in Recent English Thought." *MIND* 36 (1927): 205–210.

Seligman, Paul. "Some Aspects of Spinozism." *Proceedings of the Aristotelian Society* 61 (1960–61): 109–128.

Smith, T.V. "Spinoza's Political and Moral Philosophy." *Monist.* 43 (1933): 23–39.

Taylor, A.E. "A Further Word on Spinoza." *MIND* 55 (1946): 97–112.

Tiebout, Harry M. "Deus, Sive Natura. . . ." *Philosophy and Phenomenological Research* 16 (1955–56): 512–521.

Wernham, A.G. Review of S. Hampshire's *Spinoza. Philosophical Quarterly* 2 (1952): 187–189.

______. "Review of G.H.R. Parkinson's *Spinoza's Theory of Knowledge.*" *Philosophical Quarterly* 7 (1957): 285–286.

Wetlesen, Jon. "A Reconstruction of Basic Concepts in Spinoza's Social Psychology." *Inquiry* 12 (1969): 105–132.

White, W.H. "Spinoza's Doctrine of the Relationship between Mind and Body." *International Journal of Ethics* 6 (1895–96), 515–518.

Whittaker, T. "Transcendence in Spinoza." *MIND* 38 (1929): 293–311.

Wolf, A. "Spinoza." *Philosophy* 2 (1927): 3–19.

______. "Spinoza's Sunoptic Vision." *Philosophy* 8 (1933): 3–13.

______. "An Addition to the Correspondence of Spinoza." *Philosophy* 10 (1935): 200–204.

Index